Praise for Consulta

Sunflower Insurance Gr

"As a result of Rob Ekern's counsel, our firm has absolutely enjoyed a higher level of success. We now attract new clients by focusing on issues that erode their bottom lines."

Jim Wilson
CEO

"Our firm has experienced tremendous benefits from the Consultative Brokerage Program: including increased retention of Major Accounts, increased fee arrangements, and the attraction of new clients. Our team performs at a higher level, and we have Rob Ekern to thank for bringing us leading edge techniques."

Kristy Balthazor
Vice President of Operations

"As a producer, Consultative Brokerage gave me a way to differentiate my firm from our competitors. We have gained countless new customers."

Mark Skidmore
Vice President of Sales

JDW Insurance – El Paso, TX

"We have used C. R. Ekern and Company for over three years. We found the Consultative Brokerage concept to be a more comprehensive, teachable format than we were able to develop on our own. We've been most pleased with the results and continue to utilize all the Ekern resources."

Donald Margo
CEO

"JDW's corporate philosophy has always been to operate in a consultative manner. Rob Ekern is the first sales consultant to completely understand the subtle connectively between relationship, true value, and performance. We have increased retention, lowered operating costs, and increased our average account size."

Martin Yung
President

Talon Insurance Agency – Port Arthur, TX

"I am one of the owners of a midsized agency in Texas. After following Rob's newsletters for several years, I decided to take a more proactive approach to moving to the next level. Within a short year we are communicating with our clients at a level that was felt to be unachievable in the past. The agency is getting more referrals and compliments from not only clients but other community leaders than was ever expected. We now have a story to tell. We asked Rob to point us in the right direction and he has done so in spectacular fashion. We are total converts."

Leonard M. Forey
Managing Partner

"We have jumped into the Consultative Brokerage approach with both feet, and we are certain to have excellent results with our new and existing producers using the Ekern methods."

Mike Stroman
Sales Manager

Ag States Group – St. Paul, MN

"Ag States Group has implemented Rob's strategy and contracted with Rob to train our management team and sales force. Our client relationships have become stronger with higher retentions, and we now spend more time on genuine prospects rather than suspects."

Corwin Tufte
President

EHD Insurance – Lancaster, PA

"Consultative Brokerage provides our agency with the appropriate tools necessary to effectively quantify our services and pre-qualify prospects. Rob's methodology replaces the traditional and painful bid and quote process. How much is that worth?!"

Jeff Tompkins
President

Rutherfoord – Roanoke, VA

"Our firm has had great success with the Consultative Brokerage methodology, and we view Rob Ekern as a business partner. His contributions to the development of our sales force have been invaluable."

Kimberly Enochs
Senior Vice President

Bolton & Company Insurance – Pasadena, CA

"The Total Cost of Risk Strategy has allowed us to effectively deliver to our clients the impact of our services to their costs. Our clients now recognize how the deployment of Risk Services impacts their financial statement."

Mike Morey
Chief Operating Officer

Frost Insurance – Dallas, TX

"Consultative Brokerage translates decades of earlier attempts on how to sell consultatively into simple, practical, and powerful strategies. This is a MUST read for insurance professionals who desire to sell at a higher level."

Bruce Burdett
Regional Manager

Pritchard & Jerden – Atlanta, GA

"Our firm strongly believes in the principles and practice of Consultative Brokerage. We are committed to the client value strategy that Rob Ekern has developed."

James Bailey
President/Sales Manager

Cobbs, Allen & Hall – Atlanta, GA

"This is the best book I have ever read on our industry. Cobbs, Allen and Hall firmly believes in the Consultative Brokerage Methodology. We are pleased to be working with Rob Ekern in our continued commitment to client value."

Bruce Denson
President

"What a terrific primer for our industry. This is the American Agency System's 21st century survival guide. A 'must' read for all insurance brokerage professionals."

Bill Failor

HKMB International Insurance Brokers – Toronto, Ontario

"Rob Ekern's Consultative Brokerage process and discipline has created a subtle but effective transformation in our sales and service culture. The way we articulate our capabilities and resources to clients and prospects has been elevated; the result has been a noticeable increase in our average account size and an increase in winning new accounts."

Gregory Belton
President/Managing Partner

The Reagan Agency – Marcellus, NY

"It's a different day and age and you need to change with it to prosper. By using Rob Ekern and the Consultative Brokerage approach we are learning not only what should be done, but also how to achieve and implement it successfully."

J. Michael Reagan
President

Bollinger Insurance – Short Hills, NJ

"As one of the leading East Coast based regional brokerages, Bollinger looked long and hard for a consulting organization that would share our vision of client value. Rob Ekern and his Consultative Brokerage methodology is the one that best fits our culture of growth and professionalism."

Alex Crispo
Chief Administrative Officer

Consultative Brokerage®

The Total Cost of Risk Sales Strategy

C.R. "Rob" Ekern

C.R. Ekern & Company

This publication is designed to provide accurate and authoritative information in regard to the subject matter covered. It is sold with the understanding that the publisher is not engaged in rendering legal, accounting, or other professional service. If legal advice or other expert assistance is required, the services of a competent professional person should be sought. — from a Declaration of Principles jointly adopted by a Committee of the American Bar Association and a Committee of Publishers and Associations.

International Standard Book Number: 978-0-87218-737-5
Library of Congress Control Number: 2007929767

Printed in the United States of America

Dedicated to the bravest man
I have ever known:

Brian Failor (1982 – 2006)

"Courage is being scared to death – but saddling up anyway"
John Wayne

Table of Contents

About the Author

C. R. (Rob) Ekern

C. R. (Rob) Ekern is President of C. R. Ekern & Company. His professional background includes acknowledgement as one of the top producing brokers in North America, ultimately earning the *Willis Exceptional Producer's Award*. After 25 years of agency and brokerage management, production and client retention experience, he formed C. R. Ekern & Company.

C. R. Ekern & Company is devoted to assisting agencies and brokerages across North America in the production techniques required to produce and retain larger accounts. His firm developed the Consultative Brokerage® Methodology that is now being adopted by the most forward-thinking agencies and brokerages in North America, along with several insurance carriers.

Celebrating a ten-year anniversary in 2007, C. R. Ekern & Company provides insurance industry clients with consulting, training, and education on Consultative Brokerage® topics and techniques. For further information please visit www.crekern.com.

Preface

The Birth of a Consultative Broker

A number of years ago I found myself in rarified broker air. At the time I was in my late 30s and had recently joined the staff of the Willis Corroon Advanced Risk Management Services (ARMS). I held the lofty title of Managing Director of the National Resources Division. Pretty big stuff for a young guy who was only two years out of Fargo, North Dakota. That's right, I had started an agency from scratch in Fargo and owned it for ten years before leaving to join Corroon and Black in Phoenix (later to become Willis). But that is an entirely different story!

Nevertheless, I was fortunate to be in the boardrooms of Manhattan, the private dining rooms in London, and in meetings with presidents of major insurance carriers—the entire time making certain I got the best OJT (on the job training) available in the brokerage industry. Sitting at the feet of guys who really knew what they were doing and watching. Little did they know that I was still kicking the sod from my shoes. Hey, perception can become reality if you know when to shut up and listen!

On one occasion Willis asked me to attend a meeting of the National Association of Hotel Risk Management Directors. It was a great group of people, and I made friends easily with this relative small group of seventeen risk mangers and loss control experts. (Of course my unlimited expense account didn't hurt either!) I sat at the boardroom table with them and interacted like a seasoned broker offering advice whenever asked.

Upon returning to my office in Phoenix, I made certain to capitalize on my advantage of being the only broker at the meeting by firing out letters to the seventeen participants. Each highly crafted letter was basically identical and included this passage: "While the main business of Willis Corroon is to provide risk financing and insurance, we certainly understand the importance of loss control and claims management." Seeing as I was 2,000 miles away from my boss in Nashville, Tennessee, I made certain to send him copies of all seventeen letters. Frankly, I was pretty proud of myself for making such inroads.

At the time I reported to a fellow named Dr. Jim Davis. Jim had been one of the top educators of Vanderbilt University and ran the Willis Advanced Risk Management Services Division. The good Doctor was known as a boss who allowed his subordinates a great deal of leeway. Sometimes, it would be months between contact. But, not in this case.

My phone rang on a Friday afternoon at about 2:00 p.m. Dr. Jim was on the other end. "Rob'" he said using his best professorial tone, "I have received the letters you sent to the hotel risk managers." Then he spoke the words that changed my career forever as he slowly and precisely stated, "Your business is not to sell or provide insurance." Then he paused.

It was during that pause that my mind raced. Here was one of the smartest guys in the industry and he was telling me that my business was not selling or providing insurance! I could feel my world crashing around me; everything I had ever been taught was shattered. If my business was not providing insurance, then what was it?

Fortunately, Jim did not embarrass me by forcing the obvious question. After a several second pregnant pause he continued, "Rob, your business is to be a consultant to clients and develop a business based upon Consultative Selling. That is your ability to differentiate yourself by providing resources and helping clients reduce their costs."

It was like a bomb had gone off in my head. How do I do that? Everything I had ever known revolved around the sale and service of insurance policies. That was the beginning and the end. What else was there? How could I actually attract clients without making it about the insurance commodity? How could I demonstrate my value? How could I position myself at a higher level? How could I work with larger accounts? How? How? How?

I pondered these questions and over the course of the next five years became one of the top producing brokers in North America, ultimately earning the Willis Exceptional Producer's Award. Consultative Brokerage® was born....

Introduction

"A journey of a thousand miles begins with a single step."

Confucius

This is a book about the production and retention of larger accounts. By definition, a large account is one that has some of the following characteristics:

- A sophisticated buyer
- A potential team of buyers
- A target account in your marketplace
- Significant revenue (you decide what significant means)

There has never been a book or methodology presented to the property/casualty industry that outlines the production steps required for success in larger account production. I expect some of the concepts we discuss will entirely change many of the readers' perspectives on the production and retention of these accounts.

The basics of Consultative Brokerage® is a methodology that I began to develop in the mid-90s. At the time, I was a very successful producing broker with Willis. As you will recall, that was the depths of the soft marketplace.

I spent most of my time competing against quality large insurance agencies. What I noticed was one overriding theme when we competed:

Virtually every agency tried to make the transaction about the insurance carrier, price, or coverage.

In all honesty, the clients I chose to attract had all moved beyond those issues as a point of differentiation.

I left Willis and started a firm to assist regional and larger agencies make the transition from agent to broker. This transition involves understanding how to bring value to a client well beyond simply the insurance transaction.

At the time, there were several issues that were creating havoc in the regional brokerage industry. These included:

- The soft market had destroyed any pricing stability.
- Regional agents were losing their largest accounts through merger and acquisition of the client into much larger entities.
- Regional brokerages did not have a prospect pipeline that allowed them to replace larger accounts.

So, I developed the Consultative Brokerage® methodology to provide the most forward-thinking insurance brokerages and agencies a platform from which to elevate their production style and entire organization. Consultative Brokerage® is much more than simply a sales technique; it is a cultural shift that allows firms of any size and their producers to successfully compete.

I am happy to report that over the course of the past decade, the Consultative Brokerage® Methodology has been adopted by some of the best performing regional brokerages and several carriers. The result has been millions of dollars of revenue in commissions and fees to our clients.

Some of the issues that we address throughout the course of this book are:

- How to create a unique value proposition that will attract clients
- How to establish a business discussion with buyers that differentiates your firm
- How to effectively utilize the concept of Total Cost of Risk (TCOR)
- How to make a quality presentation and stewardship report
- How to compete exclusively on a broker of record letter

Since developing the Consultative Brokerage® methodology, I have been fortunate to make presentations to thousands of brokers. It has been gratifying to actually have a number of them come up to me one year later and tell me "You changed my life. I am having fun again in this business and feel completely different about myself."

I can't say that you will have that experience. That will depend upon how well you follow and believe the Consultative Brokerage® methodology. What I can say, however, is that I will give it my best and won't pull any punches between these pages. By the end, if you stay with me, your life as a producer, sales manager, insurance carrier, brokerage executive, or account executive may change forever.

Chapter 1

What Business Are You In?

"Show a person what they want and they will move heaven and earth to get it."

Frank Bettinger, "How I Raised Myself from Failure to Success in Selling"

So, what business are you in? Are you in the business of selling insurance, providing risk management services, or helping client's reduce their business operational costs? But, before we answer that question, let's first understand how the insurance brokerage business has changed.

That's right, I used the term brokerage. It really doesn't matter what size your organization is, you are either an agent or a broker. You can't be both with a client. The term agent identifies you as a representative of an insurance carrier; the term broker identifies you as a representative of your client. Whenever you provide clients' resources that help them reduce costs, you are acting as a broker. So, for the purposes of this book, you are all brokers. (If you intend to represent larger accounts)

So, let's discuss the evolution of the agency/brokerage industry. The modern agency/brokerage has evolved from the General Agency System of the 30s. During that period the major east-coast based insurance carriers did not have offices across the country. The time and expense of travel made it prohibitive for them to send out representatives on a regular basis. So, they set up independent businessmen as their regional representatives and gave them the pen for underwriting and claims settlement. These firms were known as General Agencies.

These General Agencies in turn worked with other subagents in their marketing territories to solicit accounts on behalf of the carriers and General Agent (GA). The subagent received a commission from the GA, and the GA received an override commission along with a contingency bonus from the carrier for underwriting profitable business.

This system worked well until the late 50s and early 60s. By that time transportation and communication had improved significantly. Also, the General Agency System had successfully helped carriers establish a foothold in various marketplaces. So, carriers could afford to change their business style. .

During the late 50s major carriers began to appoint Direct Contracted Agencies. The reason was simple: they wanted to gain better control over the distribution force.

This allowed them to better select the types of accounts they wished to underwrite, without a middle man. Many of the finest regional brokerages of today found their roots in the General Agency System.

The Direct Contracted agency model is the basis of virtually all regional brokerages and agencies. It was fine-tuned in the late 60s and early 70s. Agents were trained to compete on carrier policy forms and specialty programs. Many carriers had educational schools to assist their agents in business development. Each agent competed based upon the fine "fleet" of carriers they represented. "Judge us by the companies we keep", was the motto of many agencies as they proudly displayed their fire mark plaques on the walls of their conference rooms. Everything we did revolved entirely around the sale and service of insurance policies.

This method of business served us well throughout the 80s and into the early 90s. Those of us who survived the hard market of the mid-eighties remember how we broke it. We marketed our way out of it with carriers. As a working broker in 1986 I had a list of twenty-five potential carriers for any given deal. It included names like the Aetna (big and little), Home, Reliance, Continental, INA, USF&G, Atlantic Mutual, and Kemper. These extinct carriers, along with a number of others, led the way as we played one carrier against the other in a never-ending battle to save our clients money in the acquisition costs of their insurance program. By the way, the carriers were also willing participants in this cannibalistic death spiral.

During the 90s we were all so focused on competing on carrier and commodity price that we missed one important change. Our clients had progressed beyond seeing insurance as an important issue. As our client's business model matured, they began to understand the term "risk" went well beyond a simple hazard risk transaction. The hazard risk was the least important because they could transfer it off their balance sheets with the commodity of insurance. So, once a year they went through the insurance exercise with the intent of putting it behind them with the least amount of aggravation possible.

> *As our client's business model matured, they began to understand the term "risk" went well beyond a simple hazard risk transaction.*

The Four Quadrants of Enterprise Risk

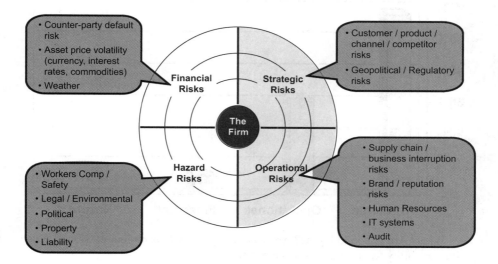

- Counter-party default risk
- Asset price volatility (currency, interest rates, commodities)
- Weather

Financial Risks

Strategic Risks

- Customer / product / channel / competitor risks
- Geopolitical / Regulatory risks

The Firm

- Workers Comp / Safety
- Legal / Environmental
- Political
- Property
- Liability

Hazard Risks

Operational Risks

- Supply chain / business interruption risks
- Brand / reputation risks
- Human Resources
- IT systems
- Audit

Why did they want to put this insurance exercise behind them? So that they could focus their energy on the real issues that impacted their business…Enterprise Risk. This term is used by the new breed of business person who understands all aspects of risk. CFOs are focused primarily in the quadrants that affect their business models, such as strategic, operational, and financial risks. They call this approach holistic because it touches the entire business operation of an organization.

Don't believe me? Take a look at the chart below. This survey reflects the importance of hazard risk in the eyes of our buyers. The question that was asked of 100 CFOs was: "What leads to the largest drop in shareholder value?" As you can see, hazard risk does not even register. Why? Because astute CFOs know that they can remove this risk from their balance sheets through insurance. They are more focused on the strategic, operational, and financial risks their organizations face.

When Companies Lose Value
Which Risk is Greatest?

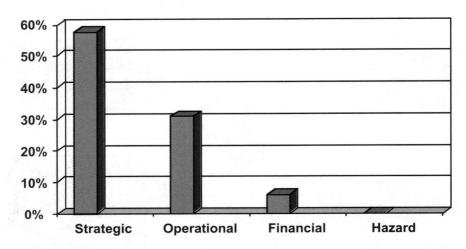

What? Are you kidding me? Are you saying that CFOs no longer want to judge us by our ability to provide insurance policies?

That's right. Now you are getting it!

When you understand the preceding two charts, you will have the answer to why some buyers hand you the packet of information and ask for you to get them bids. In many cases they don't care anymore. All insurance sellers look the same to them. They would rather spend their time running their business operations or giving the insurance placement to their friends.

But, the astute brokers of the late 90s began to change their methodology of business. They began to invest money in resource capabilities such as claims management, loss control, information services, and specialized technicians. They adopted Consultative Brokerage® as their business methodology. By doing so, they were able to align themselves with the changing expectations of their clients and prospects.

These firms do not see themselves as insurance sales organizations but, rather, as resource providers. Their sales people are not insurance agents and salesmen, they are gatekeepers of resources. Their role is to deploy these resources in order to assist clients greatly reduce their costs inside of the client's business model. These bro-

Their sales people are not insurance agents and salesmen, they are gatekeepers of resources.

kerage firms are able answer the question that all clients eventually ask: "What exactly is your value proposition and how have you impacted our business?"

When an organization and a producer adopt the Consultative Brokerage® model it allows them to translate their value to the important issues that face buyers. For instance, in the event we help a client greatly reduce their costs, we add to their profitability. This translates to the equivalent of increased sales or improved efficiencies. All of a sudden we have created a *value proposition* that focuses on the heart of a client's concerns. Now we can demonstrate our unique impact on their business.

We have shown buyers what they want . . . and they will move heaven and earth to get it!

Rob's Rule: Successful brokers are not insurance sales people. They are business consultants who help clients reduce costs.

Chapter 2

Quantifying Your Impact

"Is that all there is? Then let's turn out the lights and go dancing."

Peggy Lee, "Is That All There Is"

I n the late 90s a number of insurance carriers and larger brokers got togeth-er and formed The Quality Insurance Congress. It was to be a joint venture established to bring a higher quality of representation to our industry. This group, in conjunction with RIMS (Risk and Insurance Management Society) sponsored a survey that explains it all.

They did not see these as areas of distinction but as basics.

When buyers were asked what brought them value and what did not, the results surprised the average insurance agent. These astute buyers were neutral on the subject of compet-itiveness, expertise, and efficiency. Why? Because, as buyers they just expected it.

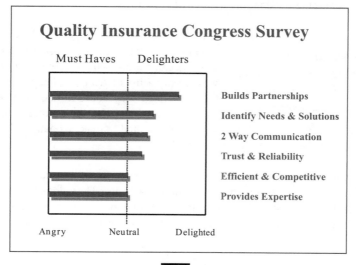

Quality Insurance Congress Survey

Must Haves   Delighters

Builds Partnerships

Identify Needs & Solutions

2 Way Communication

Trust & Reliability

Efficient & Competitive

Provides Expertise

Angry   Neutral   Delighted

They did not see these as areas of distinction but as basics. They were and still are not points of differentiation.

Yet, in many cases, one of our most used strategies for new business development is to focus a buyer on our expertise and competitiveness. No wonder many buyers get confused; we all look the same to them.

"Our firm is one of the most highly skilled insurance brokerage firms in the area," we say with some pride. "We are truly able to provide our clients with very competitive programs"

What does the buyer say in return? "OK, I know you are a fine insurance organization. What three insurance carriers do you want in order to compete for my business?"

Or, a very astute buyer might say: "Thanks for the overview of your firm. I know you are highly skilled and can obtain a competitive program. If I didn't think so, you wouldn't be here. But here is my question", he says, leaning forward across his desk, "what makes you different from these other brokers? How can I judge what makes your organization unique?"

Now, this is the point where most agents and brokers step on themselves. They will then get the buyer to agree to a Capabilities Demonstration. Brokers affectionately call these Dog and Pony Shows. In this capability demonstration the agent/broker and her supporting cast show the potential client all of the services they offer. These services include claims handling, loss control, information services, actuarial studies, and a great supporting cast. They go into detail concerning the awards they have earned and the outstanding history of their firm.

Features versus benefits are the most basic of selling skills.

But . . .they don't get the business. Why? Because they failed the most important test of any sales organization. The presentation they made was simply a list of features. They forgot to show the buyer how they could utilize these services to reduce their costs. So, their presentation looked like everyone else's and the buyer was not motivated to make a change. Features versus benefits are the most basic of selling skills.

So, how does a successful Consultative Broker® differentiate himself? How does a firm translate features into quantifiable benefits? How does a masterful sales person stand in front of a client in a presentation and say precisely and with confidence, "Over the course of the next sixty minutes, our firm will demonstrate to you how we are uniquely qualified to represent your organization. During the course of this presentation we will show you in detail how our resource capabilities will be deployed on your behalf. The ultimate goal will be to help you greatly reduce your costs and impact your business model."

How? By understanding how to present, deliver, and execute Consultative Brokerage®. One of the key elements of Consultative Brokerage® is the ability to differentiate your organization by using Total Cost of Risk. When you can do that, you will have the buyer's ear (assuming the audience really includes the buyer).

Your prospective buyers are waiting for you to adopt this philosophy. Every month, more and more astute buyers are beginning to realize that there must be more. They know that their business operations have changed, that their risks are greater than just insurance, yet they feel alone in the wilderness. Like the old Peggy Lee song, they wail "Is that all there is?"

A study done by Wausau Insurance of 200 financial executives showed a significant number of buyers were prepared to judge a broker based upon Total Cost of Risk and indirect loss costs. At the time of the survey, approximately 46 percent of the buyers found this to be an important buying factor.

The Astute Buyers are Judging Brokers By a New Measure

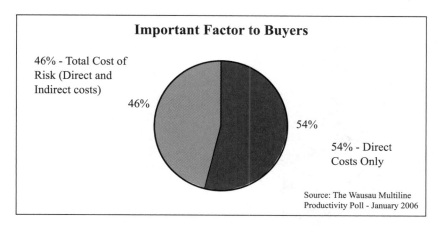

Important Factor to Buyers

46% - Total Cost of Risk (Direct and Indirect costs)

46%

54%

54% - Direct Costs Only

Source: The Wausau Multiline Productivity Poll - January 2006

How Often Do Brokers Show Buyers Total Cost of Risk

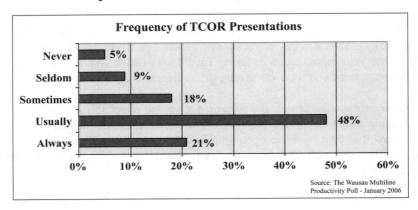

Frequency of TCOR Presentations

Never — 5%
Seldom — 9%
Sometimes — 18%
Usually — 48%
Always — 21%

0%   10%   20%   30%   40%   50%   60%

Source: The Wausau Multiline
Productivity Poll - January 2006

Yet when these same buyers were asked how often their brokers showed them their impact on Total Cost of Risk only 21 percent showed it "always." The buyers went on to rank this question in other categories entitled usually, sometimes, seldom, or never. Frankly, either you show it *always* or you don't. It is kind of like being a little bit pregnant! Also, if buyers are prepared to use it as the main point of differentiation in 46 percent of the cases and are only shown it 21 percent of the time, there is a 119 percent window of opportunity.

An Increasing Number of Buyers are Selecting Brokers Based on TCOR

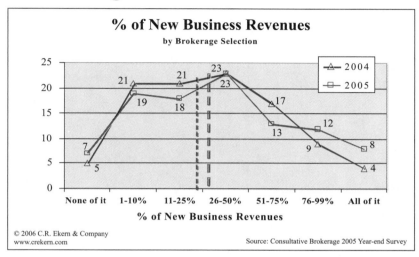

© 2006 C.R. Ekern & Company
www.crekern.com

Source: Consultative Brokerage 2005 Year-end Survey

Our own research has born these statistics to be valid. Once a year we survey the brokerage readership of our *Consultative Brokerage® Briefing™*. This publication is read by thousands of brokers across North America. When asked how they got their new business revenue, 47 percent said it came from the brokerage selection process using TCOR. That was up 5 percent from the year before.

This is not intended to become a lesson in statistics. But, it is important to separate opinion from fact. It is my opinion that brokers should base their client sales and service on the Consultative Brokerage® model 100 percent of the time. And now, a growing number of clients and brokers are in agreement.

> *...these hapless brokers will be left to bottom feed on the tainted nourishment of commodity and price.*

But, if this is the case, why don't all brokers use the Consultative Brokerage® model? Very simple, they either won't take the time to learn it, or they aren't capable of it. So, as the better, more astute clients and prospects continue to evolve ...these hapless brokers will be left to bottom feed on the tainted nourishment of commodity and price.

Rob's Rule: Features do not attract clients.

Chapter 3

The Importance of Differentiation

"They copied all they could follow but they couldn't copy my mind so I left 'em sweating and stealing a year and a half behind."

Rudyard Kipling, "Ballad of the Mary Gloucester"

It happens every day in boardrooms of brokerages across North America. A firm has (or is about to) lose one of its largest accounts. The principals of the firm are gathered to have a strategy meeting about why the client is leaving them for another broker.

"I don't understand it," the current producer says, "they have just taken our work and copied it. We had them with the right carrier and greatly improved the client's coverage. What has the other broker done that we didn't do?"

Well, here is what they didn't do: They forgot about what I call the Symmetry of Risk. Astute clients know it and the successful Consultative Brokers® are building a business model around it.

> **They forgot about what I call the Symmetry of Risk.**

During the course of the past decade or so, astute risk managers, brokers, and risk consultants have come to a conclusion regarding their Total Cost of Risk. There is a ratio between the cost of the insurance and the overall costs associated with risk and losses. That ratio is approximately, 80/20. The cost of insurance is the 20 percent!

The remaining 80 percent of clients' costs are elsewhere on their income/expense report distributed across a number of boundaries. When a claim occurs, the costs are spread across such areas as: lost productivity, loss of economic usage, administrative time, brand loss, and many others. All of these costs revolve around internal costs of loss, indirect costs of loss, and administrative costs of monitoring and implementing loss control.

Therefore, when an insurance agent focuses primarily on the policies, coverage, and price, he is only partially helping the client. He is chasing the wrong rabbit!

So, when agents tell clients or prospects that "we can save you 30 percent on your insurance", what are they really saying? "We are only going to impact your business costs by 6 percent (30 percent X 20 percent)."

Overall, these brokers provide an impact that is four times more valuable than the firms that are simply selling and servicing insurance.

However, the firms that are able to demonstrate how they will help the clients reduce their Total Costs will provide an additional 24 percent of impact on the client's financial statement. (30 percent X 80) Overall, these brokers provide an impact that is four times more valuable than the firms that are simply selling and servicing insurance.

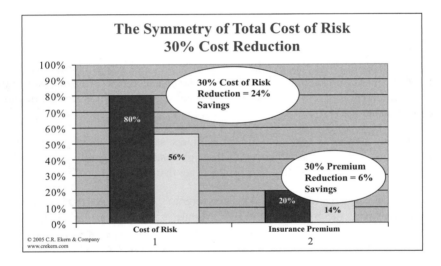

How do they accomplish this? By providing a client with resource capabilities and demonstrating how they are in a unique position to assist a client in reducing all their other costs of risk. The best Consultative Brokerages® use their resource capabilities as their main selling point.

Conning & Company produced a tremendous study that focused on the characteristics of top performing brokerages. As you probably know, Conning & Company is one of the top insurance industry research firms. It is entitled: *Commercial Insurance Brokers, They Snooze, They Lose.*

They asked the question concerning "value." They wanted to know what brokers believed brought clients the most value and allowed them to attract and retain the most highly profitable accounts.

Conning & Company Study
Commercial Insurance Brokers

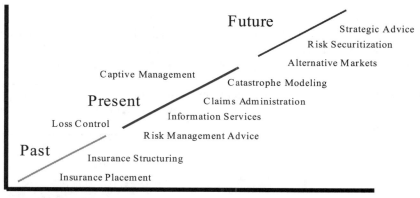

Profitability

Source: Conning & Company

Does it surprise you to learn that insurance structuring and placement ranked extremely low in these brokers' value proposition? Why do you think they placed loss control, claims, and information services as high priorities?

Why? Because as Consultative Brokers® they know the only way to impact client costs is through the application of resources. They have zero control over the price of insurance. That is in the hands of underwriters and carriers. It allows them to demonstrate how they can impact a client's costs and then quietly state . . . "Oh, by the way, we can provide you with the insurance too."

"Oh, by the way, we can provide you with the insurance too."

As these skilled Consultative Brokers® make presentations based upon the application of resource capabilities they lead the prospect to one simple conclusion. Once the prospect realizes how much it will continue to cost them in unaddressed cost of risk they have no choice. They must make a change because, *"We think we have outgrown our current agency."*

There is another very important reason that successful Consultative Brokers® tie their sales strategy to resources and Total Cost of Risk. The other agents can copy their insurance policy, coverages, and, in most cases, underwriting carrriers. However, when brokers show buyers how they can offer cost reductions through the skillful utilization of resources, they provide the buyers with a comparison based upon intellectual and business skills. It is unique, and they never give up their position and go back to insurance sales as their primary business.

With more than a little apology to Mr. Kipling, here is what Consultative Brokers® know and practice. "They copied all they could follow (the insurance policies) but they couldn't copy my mind (our firm's unique ability to provide and value resources) so I left them sweating and stealing a year and a half behind."

Rob's Rule: Another broker can copy any part of the commodity sale (policies, prices, coverages). But, they can't duplicate how you apply resources that reduce clients' costs.

Chapter 4

Resources Are the Key

"It don't mean a thing ...If it ain't got that swing."

Ella Fitzgerald

*I*n the early 90s I was a seasoned broker leading a team of experts on a prospect call in Atlanta. As we sat in front of the prospect I uttered some of the greatest buzzwords of our time. "We are a *value-added* organization," I stated with great pride. I then went on with gusto to exclaim, "Value-added, that's what our firm is all about!"

Later in the car heading away from the prospects office, one of my colleagues said with admiration, "That was masterful Rob, where did you come up with that value-added stuff? What does it mean?"

"Uh…..heck I don't know, I just made it up because it sounded good. The prospect sure seemed to respond to it!"

Boy was I glad that the prospect never asked me what I meant by the term *value-added*. Frankly I didn't have a good answer. Oh sure, I could have told them about our services in claims, risk management, or loss prevention. I could have gone on for hours about our global expertise and probably shown him a brochure for about any issue under the sun. But it wasn't the point.

When most of us talk about value-added services, we are referencing a great deal of features. They are a list of services, not outcomes. Any jamoke with an insurance license can talk about the services and features offered. However, it is entirely a camel of a different color when the producer is asked how these "value-added" services impact a client's balance sheet. Suddenly, the rubber has met the road.

> **They are a list of services, not outcomes.**

The best example of this is a meeting I attended as the featured speaker. It was a Northeastern regional brokerage's annual producer conference. As part of the festivities, they invited three major risk managers to address the group about what they looked for in a broker.

I was standing in the back of the room when one of the risk managers exclaimed, "We select our broker based upon their value-added services." I watched in horror as the entire room of brokers all nodded in appreciation of this sagacious advice. I just couldn't let this one pass without helping the group see the light.

"Excuse me," I spoke up from the back of the room, "I am a hired gun from Phoenix that will be speaking tomorrow on the subject of how to create value for a client. I wonder if you might explain what you mean by 'value added' service? How do you judge its importance?"

The risk manager who had introduced the subject sat frozen with a look of confusion on his face. I could see him struggling to identify the impact of these "services". He was rescued quickly by one of his colleagues on the panel.

"We utilized the services of our broker in the identification and implementation of a workers compensation loss prevention program. Over the course of the past three years, our broker has helped us by putting in a return-to-work policy and ergonomic lifting training. The net result has allowed us to impact our costs by $750,000 through direct and indirect cost reductions to our total cost of risk".

It is not the value-added services the broker provided, but the $750,000 of impact.

Wow! Now there is a guy who gets it. In fact, he has identified his broker's true value proposition. It is not the value-added services the broker provided, but the $750,000 of impact. Remember, it is not about the services, but the outcome. (Features versus benefits.)

It don't mean a thing...if it ain't got that swing. The swing is the amount of money a client can identify that arises from your application of resources. This becomes your quantifiable value proposition. It is what allows a successful Consultative Broker® to earn client loyalty.

As the following chart demonstrates, the Total Cost of Risk of a program that does not include resource application is merely the cost of the insurance. Unfortunately, this represents the vast majority of the insurance programs in the marketplace. The broker has simply sold insurance year after year and based his value on the marketplace or providing value added services without quantification.

Price and TCOR are the Same
Without Resources

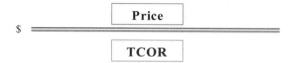

Many other brokers believe their role is to provide clients value added services. They list these services, they offer these services, but, at the end of the day, they can't tell the client the *what or why* of their importance. So, they focus on the insurance as the primary way of showing value.

Here is an important maxim that all Consultative Brokers® know, the only way to truly impact a client's costs are through the application of resource capabilities. The application of these

The only way to truly impact a client's costs are through the application of resource capabilities.

resources becomes your lever, that when skillfully applied, can provide your clients with a quantifiable result. The quantifiable impact becomes your firm's unique value proposition.

The quantifiable impact becomes your firm's unique value proposition.

As TCOR Reduces . . .
Your Value Increases!

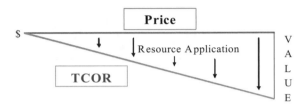

The identification, application, and quantification of resource capabilities are a cornerstone of Consultative Brokerage®. In later chapters we discuss what some of these resources are and how they should be utilized and quantified for the client. The end result will be a unique value proposition that can be clearly communicated to a client or prospect.

Rob's Rule: Never introduce a service without demonstrating what the impact will be on a client's balance sheet.

Chapter 5

Understanding Price versus Cost

"The bitterness of poor quality lasts long after the sweetness of cheap price."

Anonymous

The preceding chapters have led us to one of the most important discoveries we must accept before we go on. There is a huge difference between price and cost. The most sophisticated buyers do not really care about the price if you can demonstrate how their costs will be reduced. Successful Consultative Brokers® know this and make certain they always discuss how they will impact a client's costs.

There is an old sales adage that some of you will remember. It really sums up a buyer's experience when he purchases merely on price. Here is what it says: "The bitterness of poor quality lasts long after the sweetness of cheap price."

> *The most sophisticated buyers do not really care about the price if you can demonstrate how their costs will be reduced.*

Unfortunately in our industry it has taken a long time to explain and differentiate ourselves with quality. Now, however, we are in a position to achieve it. But, before we do so, it is imperative that we lock the difference firmly in our brains. We have been conditioned for many years to focus on the price of the commodity. Here is a case in point.

When I first started my speaking and consulting business, I sometimes fell into that trap myself. I was addressing a group of brokers located on Wilshire Boulevard in LA. I had just completed my section on the difference between price and cost.

When I address a group I can usually tell who is resisting the message. This day was no exception. In the back of the room a broker sat with his armed folded, head cocked and giving me the "where did he come from" look. Frankly, I knew I was not getting through. So, I decided to find out what he was thinking.

"Excuse me", I said politely. "My sense is that perhaps some of what I am saying may not be in agreement with your experience. I wonder if you might be willing to share your thoughts?" Smooth eh?

"Well", he exclaimed, "it is just that I don't think you understand my *customers*." He went on to explain, "My *customers* deal with me because they know I always get them the best deal. That is what they really care about."

At this point I watched the entire room begin to switch to this guy's way of thinking. In fact, I began to wonder myself if my former brokerage firm would take me back! After all, getting the cheapest price of insurance has always been our goal. What could I be thinking?

But, thank goodness, sanity returned to my head quickly. "Now see here," I patiently explained to the group, "don't you see what happened? We have been all so conditioned to accept price as our mission that at the first resistance we were all willing to agree to its primary importance."

I then spent several minutes trying to cajole this Doubting Thomas into seeing things my way. Unfortunately, I just couldn't break through. So, rather than create a running gun battle, I chose to take a break for coffee.

At the break, the owner of the firm approached me and gave me the real scoop. "You don't need to listen to him," the owner said with a smirk. "Last year he had eight clients that paid him about $400,000 in commission. This year, he has a commission base of zero. He lost all eight clients on price and hasn't attracted any new ones."

> *Yet, when we introduce the concept of cost, there is a universe of factors that can be brought into the equation.*

Oh my goodness! He was right. I didn't understand his *customers*. He didn't have any....

When we talk price to a prospect or client we are only dealing with one dimension. Yet, when we introduce the concept of cost, there is a universe of factors that can be brought into the equation—all of which can be demonstrated to clients in ways that benefit them.

The concept of cost allows you and your firm to differentiate yourselves. It leaves the door open for you not to be the cheapest seller, but to be the one to provide the highest quality. By focusing on

> *By focusing on client costs, you can elevate yourself out of the salesperson mentality and into the consultant role.*

client costs, you can elevate yourself out of the salesperson mentality and into the consultant role.

Here are the distinctions between price and cost. As a Consultative Broker® you must know, understand, and believe them:

Price versus Cost

Price

- Short Term
- Seller Based
- Product Focused
- One Component

Cost

- Long Term
- User Based
- Results Focused
- Global

Cost is the best measurement from all perspectives

This discussion is the cornerstone of Consultative Brokerage®. We have already shown you how, as a working broker, you have little control over the price or the commodity. We have discussed how the client's definition of risk has changed dramatically. We have introduced the concept of Total Cost of Risk. Now let's focus on what clients and brokers say about cost versus price.

The mega brokerages are publicly traded companies with stockholders who expect significant returns. One thing they understand is that their acquisition costs for new revenue are extremely high. So, the less dry holes they drill the better. To that end one of these brokers commissioned a study of buyers in order to understand what turned them on or off. This study was done by the Vanderbilt University Owen School of Management.

One of the important messages of this study is that buyers don't expect a broker to be the cheapest. They are looking for many other attributes in the broker they select to handle their programs. In fact, the buyer expects the broker to be the least expensive in only 17 percent of the cases.

The Prospect Says About . . . Reasons for Rejecting a Broker

- Needs not met   40%
- Competitors were better   18%
- Lack of perceived firm expertise   18%
- Cost   17%

Owen School of Management

When I began my speaking and consulting firm, I discussed this information with brokers and agents. In those days, I would ask the question: "What percent of the time is price the most important buying decision?" Invariably I was told it was the most important factor in at least 50 percent of the cases. To the astonishment of the audience, I then showed them the Owen School material.

Our firm, C. R. Ekern & Company, recently conducted our own study of brokers. The question was asked of our Consultative Brokerage® Briefing™ readership: "If you can demonstrate a reduced TCOR, do you need the lowest premium?" The results showed how far we have come in our industry.

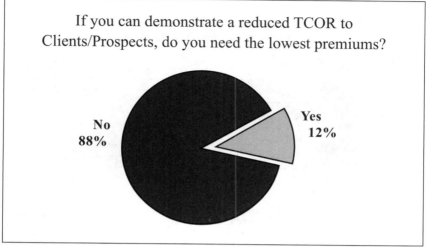

If you can demonstrate a reduced TCOR to Clients/Prospects, do you need the lowest premiums?

No
88%

Yes
12%

Source: C.R. Ekern & Company, *Consultative Broker® Briefing,* 2004 Year-End Survey

Now, for the very first time, we have brokers and buyers on the same page. Only 17 percent of the buyers and 12 percent of the brokers feel they need to have the lowest price. The vast majority are willing to meet on the common ground of cost! Wow, now we are talkin'.

> **The vast majority are willing to meet on the common ground of cost!**

But, as we showed you in a previous chapter, there is a disconnect between the number of buyers that want to be approached on a cost basis and the number of brokers that always use that approach. Why is that?

> **. . . most brokers don't have a field of vision that includes anything but price and the commodity of insurance.**

It is because most brokers don't have a field of vision that includes anything but price and the commodity of insurance._They have never been taught any other way of doing business and, when pressed, they fall back to what they know.

In a follow-up question to the previous one, we asked these same brokers to identify the most important part of a Total Cost of Risk presentation.

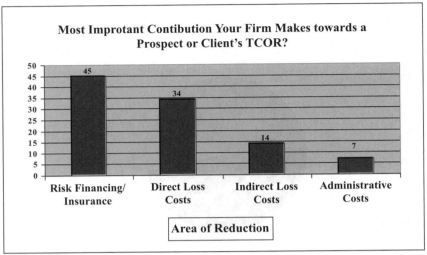

Source: C.R. Ekern & Company, *Consultative Broker® Briefing,* 2004 Year-End Survey

Almost half of the respondents told us that the cost of insurance was the most important contribution they make towards a clients cost structure. Oh, brother! Remember what we showed you earlier as regards a client's costs. Only 20 percent is the price of insurance. Therefore, while a huge percentage of brokers understand the importance of cost versus price, most of them continue to chase the wrong rabbit.

But, why is that? Most of the brokers responding to our survey represent fine quality organizations. Many of them work with large accounts and sophisticated buyers. Why would they continue to focus on the price and the commodity as the way to adjust a client's costs?

When we asked a follow-up question, the answer was made obvious. These brokers could explain the concept and identify the features of resource capabilities but were unable to translate that onto a buyer's balance sheet. Therefore, while they accepted the importance, their proposals fell flat and they reverted to what they knew. Price and commodity.

While they accepted the importance, their proposals fell flat and they reverted to what they knew.

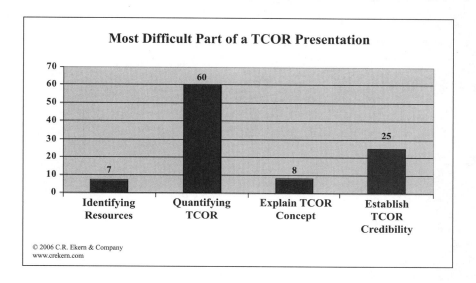

Most Difficult Part of a TCOR Presentation

© 2006 C.R. Ekern & Company
www.crekern.com

The quantification of TCOR was a significant problem, as was the establishment of credibility. The Consultative Brokerage® model was built for this very purpose. It is designed to lead brokers and their firms to the answers that clients desire. *How will you impact my costs? What process will you follow? Why are you different than the other insurance sales people that call on me?*

Rob's Rule: Price and cost ain't the same thing.

Chapter 6

Choosing Consultative Brokerage® Prospects

"It is our choices...that show what we truly are, far more than our abilities."

J. K. Rowling, *Harry Potter and The Chamber of Secrets, 1999*

When many brokers approach a large account they see what appears to be a huge cloud. They know that there is something very important inside it but are not certain where or how to reach into it. So they focus on one thing, the commodity of price and coverage.

In many cases, however, the buyer is not moved by this approach. They have seen it all too many times. Each of the brokers who calls on them uses the same tactics. "Let us review your program" they sing in unison. "We will identify the coverage gaps and make recommendations that will allow you to save money."

Or they try and wow the buyer with this one. "We would like to perform a risk management audit and cost reduction analysis." As if this isn't just another variation of the old song.

Consultative Brokers® know that it can take up to three years to write a large account. During that time there needs to be a method in place that allows you to consistently position the buyer for the next steps. So, we are not going to judge our success by the simple yardstick of "getting in this year". If we haven't done the right things, all we are getting into is a 15 to 20 percent hit ratio.

> *There needs to be a method in place that allows you to consistently position the buyer for the next steps.*

Remember our former discussion of the Owen School Study. It was commissioned to help successful brokers understand what takes place in the buyer's mind throughout the transaction. Successful brokers have a rolodex spinning constantly on the right side of their brains during an initial client call. They are trying to determine one thing, *is this buyer someone we would like to do business with?*

41

So, early on, they focus on the buyer's style in order to make certain there is a fit. They understand that as Consultative Brokers®, they just are not for everyone. It is extremely important that they develop high level consultative prospects.

In the beginning of the prospect process they look for one primary factor: Can this client become a good Consultative Brokerage® client? There are the three things they initially gauge:

*   How often does this client consider changing brokers?
*   How many brokers do they involve in their process?
*   What is the reason for the process?

Here is what the Owen School Study shows us.

The Prospect Says About . . . Frequency of Process

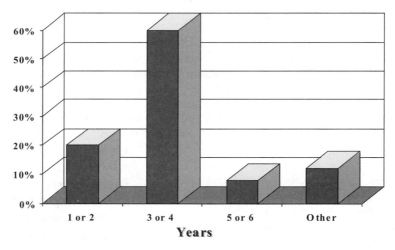

Years

A broker must be able to keep the client engaged in discussion longer that simply a renewal cycle.

The vast majority of the prospects (60 percent) will consider change every three to four years. This means that, in some cases, the Consultative Brokerage® approach must stand the test of time. A broker must be able to keep the client engaged in discussion longer that simply a renewal cycle. That is impossible to do if the dialogue is simply around the commodity and price.

Also, knowing this allows consultative brokers to target the prospects whose buying style fits their approach. Frankly, they just aren't interested in wasting time with buyers who like to keep the other guys "honest" every year or two. In contrast, buyers that only offer opportunities on a very rare basis (i.e. the current broker is the brother-law) are not considered good prospects as the time required to invest in them would place the broker out of business.

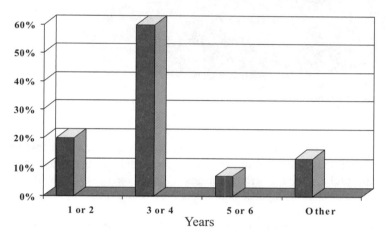

The Prospect Says About . . . How Many Firms Invited

The next important point is to understand how many other brokers are involved in competing for a client's business. What we learned is that 20 percent of the time it is just them and the incumbent broker. (Oh, that's a beautiful thing.) However, most of the time (60 percent) it is them along with two or three others. Therefore, in about 80 percent of the cases, the number of brokers is manageable.

When a client involves more than four brokers in the transaction, skilled consultative brokers walk away. They know that this type of competition is merely a beauty pageant designed to create chaos in their lives.

The Prospect Says About . . .
Why Go through the Process

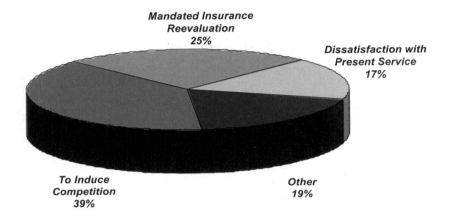

**Mandated Insurance
Reevaluation
25%**

**Dissatisfaction with
Present Service
17%**

**To Induce
Competition
39%**

**Other
19%**

This is where the rubber meets the road. Why is the prospect going through this? What we know is that 64 percent of the time the prospect is going through the process of examining brokers for the wrong reasons. (Wrong for the brokers involved.) In these cases, the brokers who participate in the process are the real prospects!

Let me tell you about the best insurance call I ever made. I was working in a major city and had been called in by the buyer of a large program. The premium at the time was in excess of $1 million. The buyer had provided me with three pieces of paper as the specifications.

This particular account was one of the major names in the city. Unfortunately, the company's insurance broker was the college roommate of the president of the company. I knew that every year, a "broker de jour" was chosen to compete on this account. The poor pigeon would then put in many hours providing a state-of-the-art program, only to have the buyer give it to the president's former roommate and current golfing buddy. The deal was so big that the company had no problem in finding a new sucker every year. Now it was my turn.

I made an appointment with the buyer to understand some of the company's issues and obtain the materials necessary to truly understand the account (other than the fact it was a big deal). The buyer indicated he would provide me with whatever information I needed.

As the appointment progressed, the buyer denied me access to quality information such as insurance policies, detailed loss data, financial statements, and loss control programs. As I asked for each, he became increasingly indignant with my intrusion into his information. As his indignation reached a crescendo, my interest in working with him decreased accordingly.

"Now wait a minute here," he hissed after fifteen minutes of my probing, "I really don't see why you need this information. We get bids every year from insurance agents, and no other agent has ever insisted on this. I know you guys don't need this information to get us quotes."

Finally, I had had enough. So, I sat calmly with my hands folded in my lap and replied with a smile on my face, "You are right, and no other insurance agent has ever written your business in the last twenty years, have they?" He threw me out of his office.

That was the best insurance call I ever made. We got right to the point. I saved myself and my family three to four months of working on a fantasy account. The buyer had us in there for all the wrong reasons, and he was incensed when he learned that I wouldn't be *his* prospect.

Remember this: as a producer you have rights. One of your inalienable rights is to select your prospects. You have the right to choose who you do business with and under what terms. If you give up that right . . . you will not be successful because many of your prospects will use you for their own purposes.

> *You have the right to choose who you do business with and under what terms.*

So, before we go any further, let's review the math. A Consultative Broker® knows that finding the right prospects can simply be a numbers game in the beginning. Let's pretend you are looking to build a prospect list of larger accounts. Where do you start?

Well, you could start just where I did several years ago. I found myself in a new city with the necessity of building a large account prospect base in short order. I started by researching 100 companies that fit my parameters of size, location, and industry type.

From that initial list, I worked the names just as the Owen Study suggested. Here is what transpired.

Initial Number of Suspects		100 Suspects
Frequency of Opportunity	60%	60 Remaining Suspects
Manageable Number of Brokers	80%	48 Remaining Suspects
Competition for the Right Reasons	36%	17 Remaining Suspects

I worked those seventeen remaining suspects by using the principles of Consultative Brokerage®. During the first six months, from a standing start, I was fortunate enough to produce three major accounts. They included a major bus operator, a $2 billion bank, and an explosive manufacturing firm. (No kidding)

By selecting the right type of buyers and knowing how to utilize Consultative Brokerage®, my production career as a major broker was secure. However, without this knowledge, I would have chased a lot of shadows and not been able to feed my family.

Rob's Rule: It's not the deals you do that make you successful. It's the deals you didn't do!

Chapter 7

Introducing the Consultative Brokerage® Matrix

"Nothing happens until somebody sells something."

Arthur H. "Red" Motley, Publisher, *Parade Magazine* (1946-1970)

B y this time, I hope you are convinced that providing value and being able to quantify our impact on a client's balance sheet is the business we are in. We don't sell insurance; we help our clients by impacting their costs.

Until now, however, there has never been a methodology to allow you—as a sales organization—to accomplish this objective. Everything our industry has ever produced revolves around the archaic business model of selling coverage and price. These two items have become a commodity.

As a young producer I was taught to seek expiration dates so I could contact prospects near their time of renewal. The purpose of this was to create "app-tivity" for the carriers. I was taught that by creating app-tivity I would prosper as long as I had enough deals in the pipeline. That was state of the art production in 1975.

Let me categorically state something that Consultative Brokers® know. X-Dates are Fools Gold!!!! They are nothing more than false security. They don't mean a thing except a low hit ratio.

X-Dates are Fools Gold!!!

Why? Because issues, problems, and client costs do not revolve around expiration dates.

I can recall being with an old time producer several years ago. I was brought into a firm because its producers were experiencing very low hit ratios and new business was suffering greatly. As I sat with this old-timer I noticed that he had close to 300 names on his prospect list.

We started to go through his list. Each prospect name evoked a reason why he hadn't written them yet. Each of these *prospects* was the name of an account he had either quoted in the past or that had promised to let him quote in the future.

After about ten minutes of squirming and discomfort on his part, I asked a fairly tough question. "How many of these do you think are really qualified prospects?" To which he replied defensively, "Why all of them of course!"

Now I am not a hard nosed consultant, primarily because I have been there as a producer and know how hard it is to make a living. But, I do need to practice tough-love sometimes. "All of them?" I questioned. "It seems to me that your actual prospect list really does not exist. What I am looking at is a list of expiration dates."

Boy, I had really touched a nerve. "Now look here", he protested, "my prospect list is my inventory. Whenever I need to make some extra money I go to my inventory and provide a quote. That is what provides me an inventory of new commissions."

He was bankrupt and didn't even know it. He was following the business model of the "insane producer". You know the one, doing the same ineffective thing over and over again, expecting different results.

When I stand in front of groups of producers I like to ask a question: What do you believe your hit ratio is when working on x-dates through quoting. The usual response is around 15 percent. Are you kidding me? What game would you play that you lost 85 percent of the time? Are you having any fun yet? Here is what the Insane Producer Model looks like:

What game would you play that you lost 85 percent of the time?

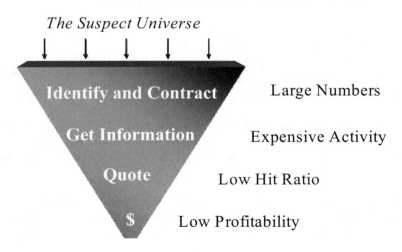

The Insane Producer
New Business Model

The Suspect Universe

Identify and Contract — Large Numbers

Get Information — Expensive Activity

Quote — Low Hit Ratio

$ — Low Profitability

The biggest fault with the insane model is that it places the focus on the sales person and the commodity. The entire transaction revolves around earning the business through having the most competitive (i.e., cheapest) price.

But here is another huge problem with the Insane Producer Model. It is very, very expensive for firms to support. Why? Because when producers work this way, they have done everything except get paid 85 percent of the time. Quality firms cannot afford this.

My best example is with a current client who has adopted the Consultative Brokerage® model. This broker repeatedly won large accounts from his main competition. How has the competitor responded? By telling prospects: "You probably shouldn't deal with those other guys, they won't get you bids like we will!"

So, the other agency is continuing to put itself out of business by working on a 15 percent hit ratio and being *selected against* by price buyers. Meanwhile our client, who is practicing Consultative Brokerage®, continues to prosper through broker of record appointments and clearly demonstrating a value proposition.

The Consultative Brokerage® model allows our brokerage clients to put the emphasis squarely where it belongs: on the client's business operations. The selling process involves positioning the brokerage as the firm that can provide these solutions to the client's problems.

> *Put the emphasis squarely where it belongs: on the client's business operations.*

Consultative Brokerage® involves three major components that lead a successful brokerage to the attraction and retention of larger accounts. Frankly, it is all about creating revenue. I have been a salesperson all my life. What I believe is this: "Nothing happens until somebody sells something." Everything in your firm exists for only one reason: somebody sold something! That is what keeps the lights on.

Here is the Consultative Brokerage® matrix; some call it The Ekern Methodology. It has been utilized by some of the top performing brokerages in North America, along with several insurance carriers.

When firms adopt the Ekern Methodology of Consultative Brokerage® it takes them to a completely different level. The purpose of Consultative Brokerage® is and always has been to allow our clients to call on and obtain larger accounts. In order to do that, certain things must occur. When it is followed correctly, our brokerage clients report an 80 percent hit ratio.

Consultative Brokerage® Matrix
"The Ekern Methodology"

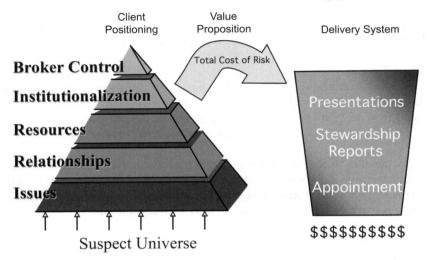

The remainder of this book will focus on the three major components of Consultative Brokerage®. These components are:

- What you need to accomplish in order to position a client into your selling strategy,

- The key elements of a Total Cost of Risk value proposition, and

- Ways of acquiring and retaining clients using our conceptual selling and stewardship report presentations.

Rob's Rule: If you want to take a higher road, then you must work at a higher level.

Chapter 8

The Five Principles of Consultative Brokerage®

"Sometimes the questions are complicated and the answers are simple."

Dr. Seuss (1904-1991)

*D*o you remember that cloud we spoke of earlier in our discussion? It masks the true keys to producing a large account. So, most brokers reach for coverage and price. That doesn't feed the bulldog.

The five principles of Consultative Brokerage® are the starting point for large account production and retention. If we skip or neglect a step, we are merely in a price competition. But, if we make certain that we focus on these five principles and keep ourselves honest in our evaluation of progress, we will ultimately be successful. (Or decide to find another buyer.)

The Five Principles of Consultative Brokerage® make up the hinge that swings large accounts and their buyers. Do not make the mistake of most amateur brokers and rush right to TCOR as your starting point. You can't get there without first focusing on these magnificent five. *TCOR is merely the point of differentiation, not a sales process.*

> ## The Five Principles of Consultative Brokerage® make up the hinge that swings large accounts and their buyers.

The Five Principles of Consultative Brokerage® *is the sales process*. How skillfully you apply it will determine your ultimate success. If you skip a step or do not fully develop each of the principles, your chances of success will be greatly diminished. You must see this as five separate parts that fit together interdependently. If one part is not positioned correctly, it will not operate at peak efficiency.

The main purpose of the Five Principles of Consultative Brokerage® is to position a buyer to accept your conceptual proposal using Total Cost of Risk. Therefore, each of these principles involves selling at its highest form. The ultimate goal is to prepare the buyer to accept your value proposition, which is developed to a more sophisticated level than that of your competitors.

> *The ultimate goal is to prepare the buyer to accept your value proposition.*

I need to stop right here and tell you something that most successful Consultative Brokers® already know. Most people in our industry are very poor sales people! Why? Because in the property casualty industry we have never had to create a need.

Can you imagine calling on a large account and starting your conversation with the words, "Have you ever considered buying property insurance?" Or how about this, "Is auto insurance something you might ever obtain?" Try calling on a hospital and asking the question, "Do you think workers compensation is something you might be interested in considering?"

The need already exists, and most insurance brokers follow that road exclusively. The ultimate competition point becomes price and commodity of coverage. They are unwilling to see a whole different road. Why? Because, in most cases, they don't have any confidence in their ability to do it any other way.

Successful Consultative Brokers® use the five principles as starting points to creating a different type of sales model. They know that from time to time they will need to educate a prospect about their value proposition and why it is vastly superior to those firms that simply provide price and coverage. After ripening the prospect with the Five Principles, they will be ready to prove their value using TCOR, with the result being appointed as the broker.

> *When a broker wins an account, it is usually because all five of these principles have been covered.*

These are the Five Principles of Consultative Brokerage®. In subsequent chapters we go into detail concerning each of them. But for now it is important to note that each of these plays a critical importance in the successful production and retention of large accounts. When a broker wins an account, it is usually because all five of these principles have been covered. When they lose an account, it is because one of these five principles has been neglected.

The 5 Principles of Consultative Brokerage®

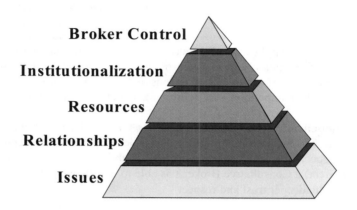

Broker Control
Institutionalization
Resources
Relationships
Issues

In a previous chapter, I mentioned how the right side of a Consultative Broker's brain is judging whether a buyer has the correct buying style. Once that is established and a Consultative Broker® has determined to work on the account, the left side of the brain kicks in. The five principles take over and are used as a guide to help "reach into the cloud'. Throughout the course of the prospecting cycle, a Consultative Broker® is constantly judging her position with the buyer based upon these principles. When she has matured the buyer and positioned herself high in each category, she is prepared to go for the broker of record letter.

Here is a short explanation of each of these principles:

Issues – Successful Consultative Brokers® are adept at understanding client issues that will lead to finding ways to reduce client costs. These issues are quantifiable and lend themselves to solutions that can be implemented through the application of resource capabilities.

Relationships – Throughout the sales process, it is important to build relationships at many levels. These are not simply friendships but are based upon a client's respect for the intellectual capital and integrity the broker has provided. The purpose of relationships is to build trust with the client so he will accept the broker's findings and recommendations as part of a conceptual presentation.

> *The purpose of relationships is to build trust with the client so he will accept the broker's findings and recommendations as part of a conceptual presentation.*

Resources – The application of resources provides a Consultative Broker® with the points of differentiation and is quantifiable when applied to the issues. It is through the application of resources that a Consultative Broker® truly can differentiate himself from the competition—by addressing a client's total cost of risk.

Institutionalization – Consultative Brokers® know the importance of establishing a business-to-business relationship. This is done by consistently communicating to the prospect or client what the firm is all about. By institutionalizing this prospect (or client) a Consultative Broker® is able to use the weight of his organization to help create deeper trust and respect.

Broker Control – This is the ability of a Consultative Broker® to effectively use the principles of Consultative Brokerage® and gain the inside track with the buyer. Someone always has broker control. The strength of broker control determines when a Consultative Broker® goes for the Broker of Record letter.

In the next chapters, we more fully discuss each of these Five Principles and how they are applied in the positioning of a prospect or client. This positioning is not a manipulation, but, rather, the preparation required for the prospect to accept and acknowledge our superior value proposition.

Rob's Rule: Selling is how you get to the stage, not what you do while on it.

Chapter 9

Consultative Brokerage® Issues – Indirect Loss Costs

"There she blows!—there she blows! A hump like a snow-hill! It is Moby Dick!"

Captain Ahab, upon seeing the sight of massive Moby Dick coming to the surface

One of the things I require producers to do in Consultative Brokerage® workshops is to identify three issues they focus on when working with their prospects or clients.

Why three? One doesn't give the client enough meat to make a decision. Two isn't enough to differentiate whether you are an expert or just lucky. Ah, but three shows the client or prospect that you have many issues you can address, you have simply chosen the three most pressing ones.

When I ask the question, "What three issues have you identified that make your value proposition unique?" the responses are usually the same. These brokers can tell me categorically how they have (or will) fix the client's coverages or selected carriers. They will say, "We have improved their business interruption coverage." Or, "We marketed their account to a more competitive carrier." In some cases they tell me, "We discovered that the automobiles were misrated." The list is endless.

My reply is, "All of that falls under one category of being good stewards of the insurance program. Now tell me two more."

Wow, does that one cause difficulties. If this is a current account and the broker can't find any other points of value, they will soon hear those dreaded words . . . "We think we have outgrown you." If it is a new account, the broker is simply chasing the commodity and will soon find herself in a bid situation.

They will soon hear those dreaded words... We think we have outgrown you.

It is time to move the playing field. Without some change in your thinking, you will continue to move the buyer into a process that is completely antiquated. You cannot show a buyer your true value unless you can quantify your impact on his financial statement. Unless the company has recently experienced an uncovered claim, it is very difficult to base your value on coverage.

One other thing. If you are working in a softening marketplace, you can't be the cheapest as prices fall almost daily. If it is a hardening market, the reverse is true. You have no control whatsoever concerning the increasing premium impact on your clients or prospects.

So, if it is not coverage or price, where are the issues? . . .Losses, that's where the real action is!

"Oh wait a minute," some of you are saying. "How can losses be the point of differentiation? The insurance carrier pays those and adjusts the premium each year to compensate for the experience. Our job is to make certain those claims get properly paid and hold underwriters' feet to the fire on renewal."

It is important for us to discuss the difference between a *direct* and *indirect* loss cost.

Do you remember our discussion of the Mercer Study? The one that showed how 80 percent of a client's costs are outside the insurance premium? Where are those costs? Much of those costs is seen on the client's balance sheet somewhere through indirect loss costs.

Indirect loss costs are the hidden (but real) costs on a client's balance sheet that are caused by expenses surrounding a claim. These expenses include a bevy of costs running the entire gamut of business expenses.

OSHA (the Occupational Safety and Health Administration) has done an excellent job of identifying the "iceberg" effect of workers compensation losses. As the following chart shows, there is a multiple to each claim that represents the hidden costs of indirect loss. Where are these costs? In the areas of lost productivity, worker replacement, supervisor time, legal expenses, and a myriad of others business expenses.

Workers Compensation
Indirect Loss Cost Factors

OSHA's Ratio of Indirect to Direct Costs

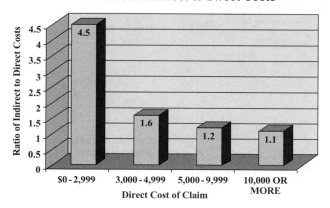

Source: US Department of Labor

So, according to OSHA, when a claim with a direct cost of $3,500 occurs, there is an additional $5,600 ($3,500 x 1.6) of indirect loss costs somewhere on a buyer's balance sheet. Imagine if you are calling on an account with $250,000 of claims. Using a conservative multiple of 1.2 across the board, the indirect loss costs are $300,000, and that is in addition to the premium.

Ok, you say. I get that. The OSHA statistics have been around for a long time under the banner of the iceberg effect. But what about all the other areas of loss? Where are the indirect loss costs in cases like automobile insurance, property insurance, general liability, or professional liability?

First of all, we must accept the fact that the traditional insurance claims handling has ignored the true cost of a client's loss. We pride ourselves and congratulate our carriers when a claim is paid quickly and smoothly. We lump that under the category of "excellent service". It is not excellent service; it is just what you and the carrier have already been paid to do. That does not make it excellent; it is merely the satisfactory fulfillment of your commitment. Here is what it looks like.

The Traditional Claims Process

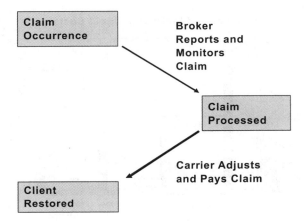

It is not until we truly understand the impact of the indirect loss costs on a client's balance sheet will we get the true cost of a loss. To ignore this is not in your client's or prospect's best interests as it is usually a very substantial cost. Also, by not addressing it, you give up your best points of differentiation.

The True Cost of Claims
Includes Indirect Loss Costs

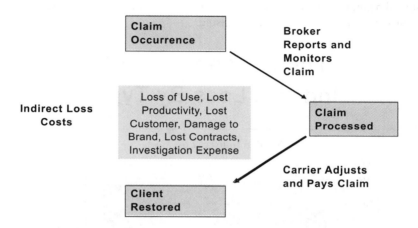

Here are some examples of how indirect loss costs can really impact a buyer's financial statement.

Automobile Losses Losing a customer or contract because of lost vehicle.

General Liability Losses Legal and investigation time, along with damage to brand image.

Property Losses Cost of renegotiating bank lines of credit when the collateral is destroyed.

Professional Liability Managerial time spent in meetings and investigation and loss of reputation.

All of these costs fall under the category of indirect loss costs. There are many others; these are simply quick examples. But, did you notice something? Each of these losses are outside the traditional insurance exposures and highly impacted the client's enterprise risk.

You may remember our earlier discussion of a study released by Wausau Insurance. One of the other interesting results of that client survey was client perception of indirect loss costs. When asked what they believed their indirect loss cost multiplier was, a growing number of them acknowledged a direct correlation between the indirect loss costs and the size of the loss itself. The following data represents the combined belief of the buyers as to the median cost of a loss by line of insurance. As you can see, they believe the costs are rising.

The Median Cost of Indirect Loss By Type

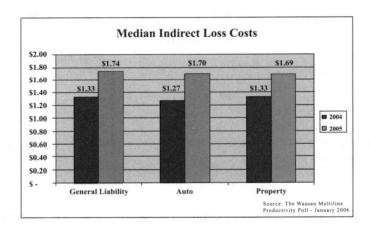

Median Indirect Loss Costs

Source: The Wausau Multiline
Productivity Poll - January 2006

By understanding the true cost of loss, Consultative Brokers® are in a position to really elevate themselves in the eyes of their prospects and clients. The main principle is this: There is a corresponding expense of some amount on a client's balance sheet for every loss. It is simply the job of a Consultative Broker® to find it, quantify it, and show the client how they can rebuild their financial performance by removing it. A business of any size has these costs.

It is simply the job of a Consultative Broker® to find it, quantify it, and show the client how they can rebuild their financial performance by removing it.

Rob's Rule: A loss of any size has a corresponding indirect cost.

Chapter 10

Issues: The Discovery Process

"Discovery consists of seeing what everybody has seen and thinking what nobody has thought."

Albert Szent-Gyorgyi (1893 - 1986)
Nobel Prize Winner

I remember sitting at the feet of a very successful broker when I first entered the brokerage world from the agency side. I had uncovered a potential large account that many brokers were shying away from. It was a massive transportation account with a great deal of losses. Frankly, I wasn't sure what to do with it because the losses made it unappealing to carriers. (I was not a Consultative Broker® at that point!)

When we discussed it, he told me something I will never forget. "The more losses the better. I love an account with a great deal of losses," he said forcefully.

What? How can that be? So, I timidly asked him to amplify on his statement. After all, if an account had a large number of losses, I would never find a carrier to compete on it.

He patiently gave me his reply. "If a client has a great deal of losses then I can truly provide him with a cost reduction. The current losses become my benchmark of indirect loss costs. By reducing the losses, I solidify my role as a consultant and gain the client for life." Hmmmm…Why didn't I think of that!

As a successful working broker, I was fortunate enough to attract clients from many industries. They included banking, construction, technology, healthcare, transportation, manufacturing, hospitality, real estate, and non-profit organizations. These are all diverse industries with one common denominator: they all had losses.

Not once did I approach any of these firms and position my sales strategy around "finding the right carrier" for them. Why? *Because, in many cases, they were with the right carrier.* If that had been my value proposition it would have kept me from even speaking with them as prospects.

A successful Consultative Broker® does not waste her time by making the deal about the insurance company. Why? Because in most cases she cannot control what happens with the carrier. She wants to put herself in a position to first prove a value proposition to the prospect and then mutter those magic words, "Oh, by the way, we can provide you with the insurance too".

Consultative Brokers® do not focus on expiration dates because those are simply arbitrary dates when the insurance contracts renew. If we are not making the presentation around the carrier and focusing on the buyer's issues, then the renewal dates are irrelevant. A buyer's issues and expenses do not revolve around the contract renewal date. (At least 80 percent do not.)

Therefore, when a prospect tells you, "My insurance renews on December 31st, please call me in September and we will talk about it". It allows you to respond in this manner:

"We understand that your insurance contract comes up for negotiation in December. However, our firm is more interested in helping you address the significant costs that are outside your insurance coverage. In most cases, these costs go well beyond simply the cost of insurance".

Well, now! In the event a Consultative Broker® really knows his business, he now has a prospect in a little bit of a quandary. What are these costs? What does this broker know that my current one isn't telling me? Perhaps I should listen a little closer to what this broker is saying to me.

First of all, let's stop here for a minute and discuss one of the major themes of Consultative Brokerage®. It is not a sales technique or trick. We are not saying these things to prospects in order to baffle them, confuse them, or set them up. Remember, it possibly will take up to three years to produce this account; therefore we need to approach the prospect with a dialogue that will stand the test of time. If this isn't the right time, then we need to have a fall back that will allow us to continue to hold our position and build on it.

The development of issues has one major goal: to give us the ability to have a meaningful business-to-business discussion. This allows us to be of value and stand our ground during a competition. Let the other firms employ their sales techniques; we will simply speak our truth to the prospect and prove our value proposition to her.

This allows us to be of value and stand our ground during a competition.

Therefore, everything we do or say from the initial call must continue to take us to a higher ground. We need to rise above the competition. That way, when the fray starts we will have already positioned ourselves differently. It is critical to our success that no matter what, we continue to hold on to our position of value and cost reduction. The minute we waiver, we will be drawn into a commodity transaction of bids, coverages, and carrier competitions.

There is what I call the *Perception Wall* inside every transaction. Unless a broker elevates his game and overcomes it, he will be lumped into the pot with every other broker in the client's eyes. However, once a broker has hurdled the wall, he is in a clear running field and doesn't have many (if any) competitors blocking the way.

Once You Breach the Perception Wall...
There's No Return

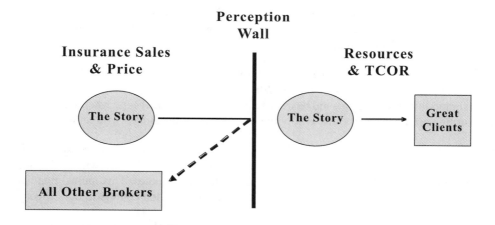

So, everything we do during the prospecting stage must lead us to a simple goal: obtaining the information that allows us to demonstrate our unique value proposition. From that point forward it is only about showing the prospect our findings and letting her make a decision based upon facts.

But where do we begin? If we aren't going to make it about the policies what do we do?

In order to act as a consultant, you must have loss data. That loss data serves as the basis for your entire value proposition. It not only provides you with the basis of a value proposition but also with a benchmark from which to compare your results (or intended results) against.

Most agents believe the only use of loss data is to provide underwriters the basis of pricing. Consultative Brokers®, however, use this information to learn the issues that are affecting a prospect or client. They know that loss data in the hands of a skillful claims analyst and loss control specialist will really give them the information they need.

There are three pieces of information a Consultative Broker® requires in order to discover the main issues of a prospect:

• The loss data

• The actual loss control program

• The buyer's financial statement

In our later discussion of Resources, I will show you how this is used to develop a quantitative value proposition. But for now let's focus our attention on what some of our clients call the *Big Three*.

Did you notice what we didn't ask for? That's right, we did not ask for copies of the policies, coverages, or prices. Why? Because we are not going to focus on the commodity and work on a bid basis. There will come at a later time when we will ask for this information, but that will only become part of the Broker of Record process.

Prior to asking for the *Big Three* we will be prepared to present the prospect with a mutual nondisclosure agreement. Of course his immediate thought will be that we are going to flood the marketplace and seek alternative quotes. This mutual nondisclosure assures the prospect that we will keep the information entirely in our office.

Oh, one other thing. By agreeing to the mutual nondisclosure, our prospect is prevented from sharing our proprietary information with any other brokers. So, it is a win/win document. Our brokerage clients that have used it find their success rate to be very high.

Here is what happens during the initial call. After the usual small talk the Consultative Broker® gets to the point. Here is what he says: "Our firm specializes in helping companies like yours reduce their total cost of risk. We have made significant impact on these clients' expense margins by helping them address the largest part of their total cost of risk."

Of course I am paraphrasing the sales conversation. However, at that point a large number of our brokerage clients have reported a strange phenomenon. The prospect begins to push copies of the policies or specifications across the table. "Here is our stuff," the buyer says in a bored tone. "Why don't you take it with you and get back to me with your recommendations for additional companies."

> *However, at that point a large number of our brokerage clients have reported a strange phenomenon.*

This is the point during which our fearless Consultative Broker® holds her ground. A successful Consultative Broker® sits back comfortably and says, "Thanks. We will get to that eventually, but for now we are interested in what really drives your costs inside your business model."

After further explanation of the total cost of risk concept and the critical importance of indirect loss costs, a Consultative Broker® is ready for the next step. In the event the buyer is intrigued (and he usually is) our intrepid broker says quietly, "I am not certain if we can be of any help to you. But, in order to find out, there are several pieces of information we will need."

In the Event You Are Interested in a Total Cost of Risk Analysis

- Mutual Nondisclosure
  - Assures Confidentiality

- Loss Data
  - Allows Claims Analysis

- Loss Prevention Program
  - Pinpoints Eliminations

- Financial Statement
  - Demonstrates Impact

For now, this is as far as our discussion on issues will go. We will address the use of this important data and how it relates to your value proposition when we get to the subject of resource utilization. So, sit tight and stay with us. More will be revealed!

Rob's Rule: If you don't have the data, you don't have a deal.

Chapter 11

Business Relationships Establish Credibility

"Relationships of trust depend on our willingness to look not only to our own interests, but also the interests of others."

Peter Farquharson, Executive Director of Habitat for
Humanity International Northern Ireland

One of the greatest skills that Consultative Brokers® possess is the ability to build business relationships. Notice I said *business* relationships. The main ingredient of a business relationship is a higher level of trust in the eyes of the buyer. This trust is based upon the knowledge, judgment, and integrity of the broker.

Now this must seem obvious to you. But the reason for creating business relationships may not appear as clearly. There is one major reason why business relationships are critical. . . If you are planning on competing conceptually the buyer must know and trust you.

If you are planning on competing conceptually the buyer must know and trust you.

In the event the buyer, or the buying team, does not know you, they will be skeptical of your presentation. They will spend time wondering who you are, why your hair is combed a certain way, or that you might do well to lose a few pounds. In short, they won't be listening to your presentation. Remember, you are not competing by using price as the method to judge your value. If you expect buyers to use a different yardstick, they must trust you.

Building business relationships and schmoozing is not the same thing.

Building business relationships and schmoozing is not the same thing. While you may have a great personality, have great seats at the game, or belong to a marvelous private country club, depending entirely on these things jeopardizes your chances of doing the deal. That is because you can't replicate the schmooze factor with all the members of the prospect's buying team or executive ranks. But, you can build a reputation with all of them that allows you to build relationships based upon a value proposition.

During my career as a broker I found that some of my closest friendships developed during the course of building a business relationship. I have observed that it is much easier to convert a business relationship to a friendship than the other way around.

There has been a great deal written and said about the importance of relationships. I am certain that many of you are familiar with the basic principles that include the dynamics of a buyer's team. (Coaches, influencers, economic buyers, etc.) Now here is the rest of the story: You and your firm must have relationships with all levels of the buyer's organization. Nobody who is involved in the process should be neglected.

What is the Value of Relationships?

- Vehicle to Establish Credibility

- Must Be Individual and Organizational

- Established at Various Levels

- Key Ingrdient to Broker Control

Let me give you two examples of the importance of relationships at all levels.

During my days as a working broker, I happened to insure a major resort that was located in the Southeast. I had never seen the property but had resolved some significant property issues simply from the plat plans of the resort. Things went well for about two years, and then one day I got "the call". You know the one.

"Hey Rob", my client left an upbeat voice message. "Give me a call will you? I've got something to discuss with you." Oh, brother. Whenever they don't leave a message concerning what it is they want to discuss, it is never good!

So, upon returning his call, I got the word. My client was in the process of selling the resort and the sale was imminent. "Thanks a lot for your great work", he praised, "Perhaps we can work together sometime in the future." I listened carefully as my $25,000 commission began to sink in the great abyss.

Of course, no broker worth his or her salt lets a great account like this just slip away. So I countered with this: "I wonder if you might be willing to introduce me to the new owner. We have resolved a lot of property issues for this resort and maybe the new owners would be interested in working with us."

My former client got back with me in several hours with the unexpected news. "Hey Rob, you aren't going to believe this, but the buyer is based in your city! The company is just down the street from your office." There is a god.

So, after one phone call, I found myself meeting with the buyer. It took me about two minutes to discover that this person was simply the executive assistant to the CFO. She had zero decision-making ability. But, she had one huge burr under her saddle. The current broker who handled the account had been treating her like she didn't exist and did not bother to see her as a business person.

So, she had been on a mission for about six months—to get the other broker fired. I was more than glad to oblige her! So, after about one month of meeting various people in the organization and consistently building business relationships, I was granted an audience with the CFO. He had already heard from several people in his organization that we were a quality firm and could do a good job for them.

The broker of record letter was signed that day. The account ultimately generated $125,000 of commission income as we added additional businesses controlled by the client.

Here is the point of this story: It took a number of meetings with various members of the firm before the deal was done. It was through the ability to develop business relationships with a number of members of the buying team that allowed us to land this big one. This business relationship included not just members of the buyer's team, but also included several of our firm team members.

Here is another one.

For many years our firm handled the insurance program of a very sizeable publishing company. This company had two distinct business entities, each of about the same size. One was located in our city; the other was located in the upper Midwest. We had been trying to represent the other entity for years.

Then one day we got the opportunity we had prayed for. The buyer called us and said, "Hey, great news, we are going to give you an opportunity to work on the account in the upper Midwest." But, before we could begin the happy celebration, he dropped the other shoe. "There is one thing, however; we are going to give the broker in the Midwest the opportunity to work on your piece of the account. We are then going to select the best broker to represent both entities." This falls under the category of being careful what you wish for.

Unfortunately, the client wasn't finished with this "great" news. He went on to instruct us, "By the way, each broker will only be allowed two presenters in the room, and the presentation meeting will take place in our Midwest office."

What a dilemma! The buyer had set things up so that we had no advantage. Instead, we were at a disadvantage because of the five-member buying team, we only knew one of the members. The remaining four were in the upper Midwest and we had never met them.

Here is what we did. As part of our "due diligence" we sent our resource team of claims, loss control, and risk management specialists to the Midwest publishing facility. For two days this team of specialists spent time meeting with the buyer's other team members. Ostensibly we were taking the time and effort to understand the risk. But, there was one other important factor at work. These people were building business relationships with the buyers.

So, at the point of the presentation, when our two presenters referenced our resource team and the value we could provide, the buyers knew the people. The buyers already felt comfortable with our team. Therefore, there was no resistance and the buyers awarded us the entire account. It generated approximately $250,000 in revenues.

In each of the above cases, the accounts changed hands because a business relationship was built. The ability to build business relationships is one of the keys to Consultative Brokerage®. For some of you, the revenues in the above accounts may seem staggering. But remember, the principles are the same, no matter the size of accounts. Business relationships allow you to keep to the high road and hold onto your value proposition throughout a torrent of competition.

Business relationships allow you to keep to the high road and hold onto your value proposition throughout a torrent of competition.

Rob's Rule: Business relationships don't make the deal, but you can't do a good one without them.

Chapter 12

Monitor and Test Relationships

"Assumptions are the termites of relationships."

Henry Winkler

As a working broker I was blessed with several quality bosses. I remember one of them saying on several occasions, "The key to success in this business is to be able to deliver bad news to the client." He went on to stress, "Anybody can deliver good news, but when you deliver the bad news you really find out where you stand."

He was talking about relationships. Strong relationships are the glue that binds a Consultative Brokerage® deal together. The strength of these relationships is a direct indicator of when a broker makes her presentation. Until the relationships are all in place smart Consultative Brokers® keep their powder dry!

Many brokers base their sales proposition on one thing . . .the relationship. They try and use it to obtain the edge on the competition in the market selection process. "They like us so much that they will give us first crack at the companies we want," they proudly crow. Or they brag to their sales managers, "They really like us and are going to let us in this year!" Oh yeah? The fact is that they are letting you in for a 15 percent hit ratio.

Consultative Brokers® know that the depth of the relationship is used for another critical purpose. It is the strength of the relationship that allows a Consultative Broker® to obtain broker control while working with a prospect. This relationship keeps a prospect patient while you obtain data, bring in resources, and do your research for a conceptual presentation.

> *It is the strength of the relationship that allows a Consultative Broker® to obtain broker control while working with a prospect.*

Your role during the prospecting cycle and certainly upon obtaining a client is to constantly ask the questions, "Who do we need to improve our relationships with?" That question has broad implications because we are talking about your entire organization. We are looking to establish those business relationships we spoke about earlier.

A successful Consultative Broker® knows that it takes much more than simply relationships to do the deal. But, the deal can get *undone* if the relationships change or are not with the right people. Here is a case in point:

Have you ever met Beelzebub? Sure you have. Beelzebub is the ancient reference to the Devil. Most of you have met him. Here is how it happened.

You just walked into your largest account for a meeting with your key contact. You have worked with this firm for several years and really have super relationships in place. Your buyer meets you in the lobby and tells you, "Great to see you. Oh, by the way, we have had some recent changes around here and I won't be the person handling the insurance anymore. We have just hired a new CFO and he wants to handle the insurance personally."

"Oh, by the way . . . Oh, by the way! Are you kidding me?" your mind silently storms. But, you fix a smile on your face and say, "Well, that is news, but I am certain we will continue to work as closely and as well with the new person as we have worked with you."

"I am certain you will", the former buyer says soothingly. "Let's go down the hall and I will introduce you. He is really a great guy; you will really enjoy working with him."

As you stand in the hallway waiting to go into the new CFO's office, your mind is numb. "What's going to happen next?" you ask yourself. The door opens and you come face to fact with Beelzebub!

You know what I mean. In that first meeting you watch your life pass in front of your eyes. In fact, Beelzebub doesn't even appear to have eyelids. He stares at you unflinchingly and unblinking as you go through your best material trying to get a personal relationship going.

"How 'bout them Cowboys this year?" You open with your best stuff as your eyes intently scan his office for any sign of personal interests you can latch onto. However, Beelzebub doesn't believe in having personal things in his office so you get no clues.

Better throw a few more lines in the water. "Do you play golf? Are you a base-ball fan? Do you have a family?" Beelzebub gives you one or two word answers with nothing else to grab.

Finally, you are exhausted; the collar on your shirt seems about two sizes too small. In this short period of time you have come to one significant conclusion . . . YOU ARE GOING TO GET FIRED!!!

Now, if all you had was a strong personal relationship with the former buyer, you are in trouble. The new CFO has an agenda and you aren't part of it. At the last three places he worked, he brought in your competition and each time he got cheaper insurance prices. So, his entire mission is to find a way to fire you.

But, here is what a Consultative Brokerage® does in that situation. Brokerage representatives will immediately prepare a stewardship report (more on that subject later) and outline for the new CFO all the ways their firm has served the client firm. They will demonstrate to the new CFO what their TCOR value proposition has been and what they are doing now. The end result is a compelling story of how the business relationship has prospered and grown through the years.

At this point your antagonist is converted because he sees the value your firm has brought. So he turns his guns elsewhere. Or, at the very least, he is neutralized and decides to fight different battles.

What makes this approach successful? First of all, your firm clearly understood the value of your business relationship so, when required to describe it, you were able to do it. Second, you took the initiative and proved your value in a succinct business discussion. Third, Beelzebub has learned that you are strong enough to stand up for yourself. Believe it or not, some clients put you to the test for that very reason. Their thinking is that if you can't stand up for yourself, you won't be able to stand up for them!

Consultative Brokers® know that relationships must be constantly monitored throughout your client's or prospect's firm. When something changes, they take the initiative. They don't wait for the client to question them, they anticipate. They are able to demonstrate their value on a short notice because they constantly ask themselves, "What value have we brought our client?" This thinking has become second nature.

Whether on a new account, or a current one, successful consultative brokers are constantly testing the strength of their relationships. This is necessary because, as these relationships grow or shrink, so does your ability to exercise broker control. Also, these relationships are constantly changing as the prospecting cycle matures.

Why must you test relationships?

* The strength of the relationship is the best indicator of your perceived consultative value

Many brokers do not put their relationships to the test during the prospecting cycle. Why? Because in many cases they don't want to know the answer. In these situations they are not confident that their relationship is based upon anything more than simply providing the buyer a price. Therefore, they don't have a basis for testing the relationship for fear of being excused from the competition before they get a chance to quote.

But, a Consultative Broker® chooses her prospects. She is working a methodology that requires a prospect to cooperate with her requests and respect her recommendations. In order to work successfully, she understands that the prospect must put some "skin in the game"

"Skin in the game" describes actions on a prospect's part that he probably doesn't perform for every other broker. Understanding how to test a prospect's skin is what separates the amateur brokers from seasoned professionals. It is not a negative action; it is not something that is adversarial. Very simply, these brokers have expectations.

If you remember nothing else from this section, remember this: As a producer you have rights. One of your unalienable rights is to expect a prospect to meet you at least half way. As a producer, you have no way to know what the prospect is really thinking about you and your firm unless you test them. The answer will determine whether or not you proceed.

One of your unalienable rights is to expect a prospect to meet you at least half way.

So, Consultative Brokers® are very skilled at asking for and obtaining actions from prospects that allow them to determine whether they are beginning to obtain broker control. Here are some of the things that they regularly request or require from their prospects:

How do you test relationships?

- Ask for Information

- Invite to Events

- Request Regular Meetings

- Invite to Office

- Ask for Referrals

- Put Skin in the Game

Prospect Financial Information – Have you ever wondered why astute underwriters really like to see a prospect's financial information? Not only for the obvious reason of understanding their business operations. Nope. They want to see if the broker can actually obtain it! The ability to get the financials subtly indicates that the broker has or is beginning to gain control on the account. After all, somebody probably has it. So if the prospecting broker can't get it, she probably won't do the deal.

Invitation to Events – Smart brokers know that in many cases they must convince a buyer that they are after more than simply the deal. Therefore, they are willing to demonstrate to prospects an interest in knowing them outside of the professional environment. Later, if they work together as broker and client, it will be important that this bond is established to work through tough situations. (That inevitably occurs.) If these invitations are spurned by the prospect, a skilled broker questions the intentions of the prospect.

Request Regular Meetings – A true barometer of your consultative value is the amount of time a prospect is willing to grant you. Of course, this presupposes that the basis of each meeting is the dissemination of valuable information that the prospect will find useful. By requesting regular meetings and making them meaningful, a Consultative Broker® is supplanting the current broker as the "go to" source for current information.

Invite Prospects to Your Office – This is one of the best techniques that is utilized by successful Consultative Brokers®. A skilled broker uses this as an indicator of which way the prospect is leaning. If the invitation is accepted, she knows the prospect is intrigued. She then will use this opportunity to introduce the prospect to various other members of her firm, thereby creating an additional level of relationships.

Ask Prospects for Referrals – One of the best ways to judge your value to a prospect is to request referrals. In the event he provides them, you know that your position is becoming solid. While this may seem being forward by some brokers, a seasoned Consultative Broker® knows this is the one of the best tests of all.

All of these techniques for testing relationships will require that prospects put some skin in the game. In the event a prospect rebuffs these attempts, a Consultative Broker® knows he has a great deal of work left to do. It will be imperative that the prospect sees him differently from the other brokers. This will be critical at the point of presentation because it will be a conceptual presentation, and the strength of the relationship will determine the buyer's confidence in the anticipated impact.

Strong relationships are vital if you intend to compete conceptually and be chosen as the broker. Such relationships answer the questions: "How do we know that we can trust you?" or "Why should we believe what you are telling us conceptually?" or "Who says so?" If you have strong relationships in place, these questions will not become an issue.

If you don't have strong relationships at several levels the buyer will revert to the yardstick he knows best. This is the yardstick that takes you out of the equation and places it back where you are most comfortable: the price and the commodity.

Rob's Rule: Always keep your eyes on the horizon for changing relationships.

Chapter 13

Become a Gatekeeper of Resources

"Your true value depends entirely on what you are compared with."

Bob Wells, American editor for Windows and .NET Magazine

The ability to provide and utilize resources is the key element of the Consultative Brokerage® process. This is a process that is foreign to most producers because they were never taught the importance of resources as a method reducing buyer's costs. In fact, most of them believed the opposite. They thought resources, in many cases, were the enemy!

Think back to your beginning days in the insurance sales careers. You had just landed your first large account by obtaining a tremendous price offering from one of your insurance companies. Now it begins. The never-ending flow of paper from this carrier's loss control department. Recommendations for this, recommendations for that. What the heck do "back braces" have to do with the price of tea in China anyway?

So, as an agent who is protecting his client from predatory underwriter pricing, you learned early in your career to return these recommendations to the underwriters with the heading, "Are in process of implementing", or "Are under consideration". Whew! You dodged another one until next year. After all, the only reason for these nuisances is so that the insurance company can document its files.

But here is the problem. By not providing resources, you have done nothing to differentiate yourself other than provide a price and coverage from a carrier. In many cases, your competition represents these same insurance companies. When your competition finds out you have done nothing other than provide insurance, you will eventually hear those infamous words: "We think we have outgrown you."

So, now, many of the leading regional brokerages are providing their own resource capabilities. The successful firms and their producers are focusing on ways to deploy these resources and value their impact. They understand the importance of demonstrating the *True Cost of Risk* and how their firm can provide value.

Before we go on, I believe a word is in order to those of you who do not have the resource capabilities of a large regional brokerage. In this case it is imperative that you look toward your best insurance carriers for assistance. Make it a point to learn exactly what their resource capabilities are. Spend time focusing on how you and your firm can utilize these capabilities and be perceived as a gatekeeper of resources.

Whether you have the resources on staff or must obtain them elsewhere, the concept is the same. In order for you and your firm to have value, buyers must perceive you as a *Gatekeeper of Resources*. This is an entirely different model from the traditional sale and service of insurance policies. Frankly, it is the only way you can develop a lasting business relationship with a client.

In the traditional model the broker's role revolves entirely around the insurance policy. These brokers negotiate the terms and conditions of the coverage and then deliver the policies, service the endorsements, and, in some cases, report claims. The remaining functions of loss control and claims management are abdicated to the insurance carrier.

The Traditional
Client Service Model

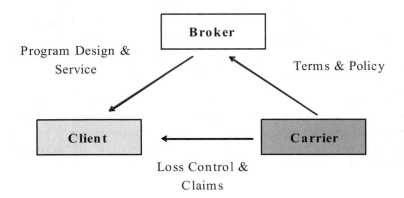

This model served our industry well for a number of years. However, with the development of sophisticated loss control techniques, claims compression tools, and the client's thirst for information, this model is now archaic. More importantly, not only is it archaic, but it is ultimately broker suicide.

What happens when you as the broker abdicate your responsibility and interest in the delivery of resources? You become invisible. Woe be to the Invisible Broker. Eventually, you will be fired by fax! (Or blackberry!) You have lost your value inside the transaction. Your client, or prospect, sees you as the expendable part of the equation.

In the Traditional Model . . .
The Broker Becomes Invisible

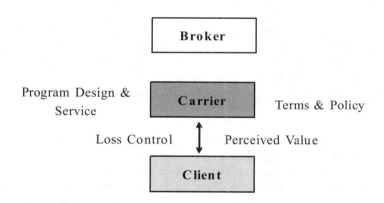

As a working broker I was fortunate to represent programs for a number of hospital organizations. At the time, there was a specific carrier that excelled in the placement and service to that industry. So, as a conscientious broker, I made certain this carrier represented one of my clients. But one little problem developed . . .

Throughout the course of the year I continued to receive copies of correspondence between my selected carrier and my client. This carrier had called meetings, offered direct assistance, and even arranged special presentations with my client. All without my knowledge until after the fact. The bubble burst when this carrier arranged a meeting with the hospital CEO without including me.

Now some of you might say, "What's the problem? Here is an example of a carrier doing all the right things on your behalf." But, that is not the way a Consultative Broker® would react. A successful broker would see this as an attempt by the carrier to usurp the broker's relationship and make it about the carrier's resources and relationship.

Now in fairness to this specific carrier, most of the time its agents and brokers had no interest in making certain the loss control was implemented. Nor did they have an interest in sitting at the table while the client's claims were being reviewed and analyzed. So, in order to make certain it provided the outcome as promised, this carrier consistently took matters into its own hands. Agents and brokers could come and go, but this carrier always retained the business.

It took me about two months to realize that I would be on the outside looking in without something changing. If this were to continue, the only role I would have would be to deliver the renewal pricing. Ultimately, the client would see us as an expensive "frictional cost" that brought nothing to the table.

There was one other thing that concerned me. It was my business reputation and that of my firm's that was on the line. On a significant account, it behooved me to have a strong presence. Things were going well with the implementation of loss control and claims; we needed to be perceived as having some impact on this outcome. Lord knows, other things can go wrong and, if we were to blame for that, we needed the credit for the good stuff!

So, after repeated attempts to convince the carrier I would not tolerate being outside the loop on my own deal, the carrier representative finally forced my hand. What happened? Well, you guessed it. I fired that insurance company from the account and replaced it with a carrier that was willing to see us as a valuable partner. Frankly, we were. This client continued to receive excellent results with a different carrier. In fact, our reputation became so good that we ultimately represented six other hospitals in our marketplace.

It is imperative that your clients and prospects see you as a gatekeeper of resources, regardless of whether that be with your own internal resources or those of your carriers. That is where your long-term value lies. But, there are very few brokers who understand how to differentiate and quantify their value through the deployment of resources.

Now I know what some of you may be thinking: "My role is to create new clients and retain the ones I have. How can I spend time on this also?" Or you may

The Consultative Brokerage®
Gatekeeper Model

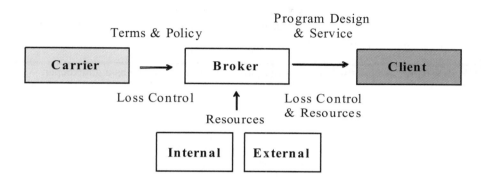

be saying: "I don't really know much about loss control specifics and really don't care about things like ergonomics or claims reserving."

Here is my answer: You need to see this as part of your role as a steward of your client's risk expense. If you don't take an interest, someone else will on large accounts. You must think of this as part of your selling and renewal strategy. When you do, your life will change. No longer will you be on an adversarial basis with your clients as you approach the renewal date. You will be their partner, with only one objective, to help them select the best carrier for their renewal project. That carrier will not necessarily be the cheapest.

As regards the knowledge question: You are not expected to be an expert in the various loss control and claims handling techniques. But, you do need to be an expert in knowing where to find them, how to display them to the client/prospect, and how to value their impact at the point of sale, renewal, or stewardship report.

As a working broker, I was fortunate enough to cross a number of industry boundaries in my client base. It ran the gamut from an explosive manufacturer to a major banking institution. It included technology, healthcare, construction, non-profit, hospitality, aviation and transportation. This was a diverse group of industries that all had one thing in common: the need for resource capabilities to assist them in reducing costs.

While all the other brokers spent time finding the right insurance company, (i.e. cheapest) I spent my time ferreting out the top resources in each of these industries. Therefore, I was able to be perceived as a very valuable partner. It allowed us to say, "Oh, and by the way, we provide insurance too."

The deployment of resources requires that you and your organization understand the importance of being perceived as a gatekeeper who brings value. Whether you have these resources on staff or must obtain them elsewhere, the time, expense and effort will reap tremendous rewards.

Rob's Rule: A client will never fire a broker that brings value as a gatekeeper.

Chapter 14

Introducing "The Four Quadrants of Resources"

"One that would have the fruit must climb the tree."

Thomas Fuller
English clergyman & historian (1608 – 1661)

I still remember the day I made the transition from small market agent to a broker. I had been with Corroon and Black for about eight months. My success was marginal. The transactions I had done were all of a commodity nature based upon price and coverage. Frankly, I was not having any fun at all.

The main reason for my frustration was the fact that no matter what I did, I was running into the teeth of other local insurance agents in my marketplace. In most cases these agents were long-time residents of my area and I couldn't compete with their established relationships. So, like every other gunslinger I was trying to get into the door based upon price and markets.

So one day, in a last ditch effort, I decided to do something different. I went into the supply room and took a brochure for every program and resource that our firm touted. There were probably twenty-five different brochures on subjects ranging from risk financing to environmental expertise.

I sat down with these brochures and asked myself one question, "What is the common denominator of all these programs and offerings?" I supposed somebody smarter than me had already figured that out, so why not look for the golden answer. It took several hours, but the answer finally came.

Each of the offerings of these brochures revolved around one thing . . . resource capabilities. It was the goal of each of these brochures to explain to clients and prospects how our firm could provide them resource capabilities in order to help them reduce costs.

Each of the offerings of these brochures revolved around one thing... resource capabilities.

So, as a producer, my role should be to demonstrate how these resources can be utilized.

AHA!!! So, as a producer, my role should be to demonstrate how these resources can be utilized. Perhaps that would give me an advantage over the other insurance agents in my marketplace that were just selling price and coverage. Hmmmm, I wonder?

Now there is one little stumbling block to this approach. I didn't know myself how to use these resources. Oh sure I could spout out the advantages of risk management, loss control, claims management, and several other resources; but I didn't know how they really operated. So, the quest began.

If I intended to use these resources as points of differentiation, I needed to be able to explain them in a fairly simple manner to prospects who had never been introduced to them. Also, it was important that I be able to utilize them in a format that could be replicated from one prospect or client to the next.

This led to the development of a tool I call the "Four Quadrants of Resources". When utilized properly, it shows the buyer how a firm can deploy resources in order to reduce costs. Also, it becomes the roadmap for any broker that is attempting to analyze what capabilities must be deployed.

Here are the Four Quadrants of Resources. When a Consultative Broker® understands how to use them they can stand toe to toe with a brokerage firm of any size.

The Four Quadrants of Resources

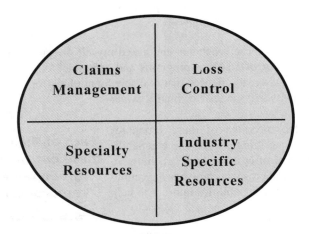

First of all, let me make one thing clear. These resources all fall under the banner of risk management. To really understand how to use them, a successful Consultative Broker® should broaden his horizons through some of the excellent risk management education programs that exist. But, whatever you do, do not fall into the trap that snares many agents. A risk management program and an insurance program are two entirely different things. If you are going to assist a client in the area of risk management, you must understand how to utilize the Four Quadrants.

Here is another thing to remember. The Four Quadrants are not mutually exclusive. Each of them has an interrelated impact on a client's costs and program. In the event you neglect one, you will not have accomplished the entire job for your client or prospect. Unfortunately, this will leave the door open for a competitor that understands how to work with the entire picture.

The Four Quadrants of Resources are the answer that most agents and brokers miss. They see these as unimportant to the sale of insurance. Of course they are right! The effective deployment of these resources and the quantification of their impact have nothing to do with the sale of insurance. They revolve entirely around reducing a client's costs and helping a Consultative Broker® build a value proposition.

One last caveat before we move into the Four Quadrants. Whenever you are working with a resource, remember these things:

1.   You must know what you intend to accomplish with a client. Do not expect your resource to accomplish the deal. At the end of the day it is still your responsibility to close it.

2.   Keep your eyes on the prize. The deployment of resources should keep you moving forward into the sale. Don't get bogged down with all the technicalities; let your resource handle these.

3.   Keep your resource representatives informed. Do not treat them like unimportant members of the team. Your prospect will sniff this out and sense mistrust on your part. This will lead to a vote of no-confidence in you.

As some of you read the following chapters you may become intimidated. Frankly, those of you in smaller organizations may not have these resources readily at your disposal. Well, don't fret. A smart broker has the ability to obtain them from outside resources. In some cases, where you get them is not the point, it is the fact that you have the ability to get them and the skill to use them that counts.

Rob's Rule: Client cost reductions revolve around the Four Quadrants of Resources.

Chapter 15

Claims Management & Loss Control Resources

"An investment in knowledge always pays the best interest."

Benjamin Franklin

B efore going too far in our discussion, it is very important that we all agree on the push-pull of claims management and loss control. In a nutshell, here it is. Claims management can be used to change a client's experience going back in time; loss control is used to generate a positive outcome going forward. You can't use one without the other and achieve the desired effect.

The Push-Pull of Claims
Management and Loss Control

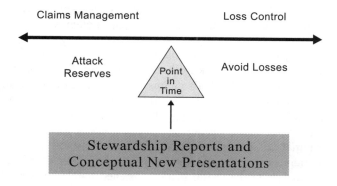

Consultative brokers are very astute at demonstrating this to clients and prospects. They do so by showing the *prospects* conceptually how they will impact their Total Cost of Risk. They show *clients*, through stewardship reports, how they have and will continue to reduce TCOR.

The key to each of these is the same; to reduce and avoid loss costs. If the client has a loss sensitive program—including deductibles, retrospective rating, dividend plans, or self-insurance—these loss costs are incurred on a direct basis. Whenever these costs hit the insured's financial statement through lost productivity or lost economic opportunity the costs are indirect. Whether they are direct or indirect, however, your role as a broker is to demonstrate how your resources can reduce these costs.

Claims Management

For the purposes of this discussion, we are not speaking about the effective ability to process claims. While this is important, as you will recall, the Quality Insurance Congress determined this was not a point of differentiation. (Efficiency was expected.) Rather, we define claims management as having the ability to impact the outcome of the claim through case reviews, adjusting techniques, and closure.

Remember our discussion on indirect loss costs. What happens if we are able to impact the ultimate cost of a workers compensation claim? For every dollar by which we reduce the ultimate claim, there is a multiple impact from these indirect loss costs.

But, how can we reduce the costs of the claim? They are reduced by attacking the reserves through active claims management. A skilled claims manager has the ability to study a file and determine any number of ways a reserve can be reduced. Examples of this would be implementation of a nurse case manager, subrogation, investigation, return to work programs, and medical networks. Any changes that can be made on the reserve cost and the claim will impact a client's Total Cost of Risk.

Here is a case in point. As a working broker I was called in to help a regional hospital organization. The hospital's workers compensation costs were dramatically increasing. Based upon the hospital's claims history, the experience modifier had risen dramatically along with the premium. In the era of managed care, the executive in charge of the program was mandated by the board to get things back in line.

After our initial call, the prospect gave us access to the loss data. I in turn made certain that our claims management expert gave these the once over. Whoa!! What's this!! The loss data showed a claim that approached $400,000, virtually all of it reserved for indemnity. (Paying the injured worker lost wages over time.)

Now, because our claims management expert had experience in reviewing and closing claims, we got permission to review that particular file. The claim involved a janitorial worker who was using chemicals to clean a surface. He stood over the bucket and got a big whiff, and, unfortunately, his lungs were severely damaged.

What our claims management expert discovered was that the current carrier had grossly mishandled the claim. The carrier had neglected to do what (at that time) all workers compensation companies regularly practiced in that jurisdiction. The carrier did not subrogate the claim against the chemical manufacturer. Had it done so, the claim may have been removed from the client's experience.

So, upon being appointed as the broker, the first thing we did was use our claims management expertise to have the claim removed from the loss data by working with the carrier and obtaining subrogation. Several good things happened immediately for the client:

1.   The experience modification dropped tremendously

2.   The account became much more attractive to underwriters for credits

3.   The indirect loss costs were reduced by $440,000!

Hold on! What is that last part about $440,000? Yes, Virginia, I said $440,000. That number is a reflection of the OSHA statistics that show for every dollar spent on a claim over $10,000 there is a direct correlation of $1.10 for each dollar expended ($400,000 X $1.10 = $440,000).

So, for a hospital in a managed care environment, where the capital budget revolved around a 2 percent or less contribution to surplus, we made a big splash. Our efforts had the effect of providing the client what otherwise would have required a $22,000,000 infusion of revenue ($440,000/.02 = $22,000,000). Now that is a lot of gauze and bandages!

Some of you reading this may say, "Well, that is all good, but I don't have access to a good claims person." Of course you do. At one point in my career I didn't have a person on staff, so I found a claims person that I could work with on the staff of our leading carrier. You can do that, or you can find a very good independent claims adjuster and retain her.

Loss Control

Loss Control is one of the most misunderstood disciplines inside the brokerage industry. Most agents see loss control as an aggravation. Historically, they have been used to responding to loss control recommendations from carriers. These recommendations in many cases are seen as intrusions into a client's business operation.

Unfortunately, in these situations, the carrier's underwriter is using them as a way of making the account conform to underwriting guidelines. So, this places the carrier, client, and agent in a contentious position.

Astute consultative brokers see things in a different light. They understand that when a client invests in loss control, there is a return on investment (ROI).

I am constantly asked by brokers, "How do we really show the client the value of our loss control efforts?" Here is my answer. You show it to them two different ways, depending upon the type of presentation you are making.

1. If it is a current client, and the losses have been reduced because of your efforts, show the company what the indirect loss costs were before your initiative began. Quantify the impact of these on the buyer's financial statement and show the difference. This is your value proposition.

2. If it is a new prospect, show the impact your loss control efforts can achieve. How? By understanding the industry statistics that qualified loss control experts already know. There are a number of industry statistics that demonstrate the expected results of successful loss control programs on a client's losses. It is simply a matter of extrapolating these statistics against the current loss picture and showing the buyer the difference. This will become your target value proposition. (More on this later.)

Once brokers are able to demonstrate the impact of their loss control efforts, they are able to really differentiate themselves. But here is a warning: If you show loss control resources to prospects you had better be ready to deliver them. The insurance brokerage world is littered with bodies of brokers who sold prospects on their capabilities and then failed to deliver them.

> *The insurance brokerage world is littered with bodies of brokers who sold prospects on their capabilities and then failed to deliver them.*

This is not intended to be a tutorial on the various loss control techniques that are available to clients. You should have that discussion with the best loss control expert to whom you have access. Remember, you are a gatekeeper of resources, not a one-man band!

The purpose of having a copy of the current "actual" loss control program is to develop a benchmark. Either the benchmark is the current program and what is or isn't working, or it is what the client should be installing. Understanding the current program is critical to your success. It allows you to differentiate yourself with an outcome (i.e., the results on the buyer's financial statement).

Oh, but I can hear some of you now. "I tried that once with one of my largest clients," you say. "I told the buyer that if she improved her company's loss control programs, she would really reduce losses and save her company money. When I informed this client that it would cost her $30,000 in loss control expense, she lost interest."

Well, here is my answer. Of course she lost interest. She saw this investment as an expense, not a positive return on investment. If you were like most agents or brokers you showed how the loss control would help you get a better rate on the company's insurance policy. Not, how it would impact the company's business model.

I was recently working with one of our brokerage clients. The broker had just delivered a stewardship report to one of his current clients. He demonstrated how the loss control efforts had decreased the buyer's costs by $300,000. During the stewardship report he informed the client that in order to keep the loss control current, the company needed to invest $30,000 in additional expense.

The CFO, being expense conscious, declined to spend the money. This brokerage client came to us and asked: "What do we tell this CFO in order to convince him?"

My answer: "Tell him that he is risking the $300,000 in cost savings against the $30,000 expense. Explain to him that you cannot guarantee this kind of savings performance in the future without the additional loss control. In fact, if you continue to work with him and he chooses not to implement your recommendations, have him sign a waiver that will protect you against future blame when his program deteriorates and his costs increase."

Hey, you either believe your own recommendations or you don't. If you believe them, then you need to be ready to put your reputation on the line. If you are just selling insurance, then it won't be important, as you will eventually have to find another client anyway!

There does come a time when you as a working Consultative Broker® will need to stand your ground regarding loss control implementation. Occasionally, you will need to practice tough love and force the client to take action. If you don't, you will not have a value proposition later on down the road.

I was speaking to a group of producers with a client firm based on the West Coast. When we got to the discussion of resources, one of the producers recounted a current situation he was having with one of his largest clients. "I think we are in good shape," he proudly announced to the group. "I have continued to offer our loss control services and the client has just not taken advantage of them. So, I am protected on the renewal because we offered and client didn't accept."

Hold on Sparky! Here is the perspective of a Consultative Broker®. You are in trouble on this account and don't even know it. Eventually, something bad will happen. When it does, you will get the blame. I have never met a buyer yet who said to his boss: "Yeah, I am the reason our costs just went up considerably. If I had just listened to our skillful insurance agent, things would be different for us. I am really to blame for this financial catastrophe."

What happens in the real world is that eventually the hapless insurance agent becomes the scapegoat for the client's own business decision. At the very best, the agent/broker can never prove a value proposition and will be forced to retain this account by price competition.

So, here are some closing words on loss control. As a successful broker you must understand how to generate an outcome for clients. This outcome is not the action itself, but the return on investment. Don't fall in love with the implementation or the process; while these are important, they are just features. Your role as a professional Consultative Broker® is to use these resources to create a quantifiable value so a client can see the return on investment as it relates to TCOR.

Rob's Rule: Always show the ROI of a loss control program.

Chapter 16

Specialty and Industry Specific Resources

"Talent hits a target no one else can hit; genius hits a target no one else can see."

Arthur Schopenhauer
German philosopher (1788 - 1860)

The utilization of the final two resources of the Four Quadrants requires that a Consultative Broker® really understand a client's business operation. These resources will take an astute broker to the next level inside a client's business model by providing quality information and services that eventually become indispensable to the client.

The usage of these resources is laser-like in its application. When properly applied and utilized, these resources will provide the Consultative Broker® with not only a value proposition but also a huge exit barrier. Once the client integrates the resources into her operation, she will be reluctant to change brokers.

These resources will provide the Consultative Broker® with not only a value proposition but also a huge exit barrier.

Specialty Resources

Specialty resources are used by successful brokers to address specific client needs as they relate to high level information. While claims management and loss control require action, the delivery of these resources demands that a broker understand how he can change a client's experience with information.

Until recently, specialty resources were reserved entirely for the mega brokerages. These firms have a number of experts on staff that provide clients with the ability to reduce costs in many areas. However, with the continued improvement of technology, a number of independent vendors have appeared that will help a brokerage of any size provide clients and prospects with quality information.

I am often asked for examples of these specific specialty resources and how to use them. As most of them are proprietary and operate under trade names, I will leave it up to the reader to fill in the blanks with the specific trade names and instead discuss what they do. Here are three popular examples:

Workers Compensation Modifier Projection Software

These programs allow brokers who understand the push-pull of claims and loss control to demonstrate how they can change clients' workers compensation costs. Once the impact on losses is determined, these brokers have the capability to plug the new data into the experience modifier calculation formula and see how it will be impacted. The use of these programs is extremely effective in not only servicing accounts but also creating conceptual sales that demonstrate the potential impact of your firm.

Premium Benchmarking Services

Historically, benchmarking has been reserved for only the very large accounts. Through the auspices of RIMS (Risk and Insurance Management Society), risk managers for large corporations have shared data on their accounts for years. Independent brokers now have the ability to provide clients premium benchmarking and limit comparisons on much smaller accounts.

While these services do revolve around primarily the sale and service of the policies, they do help an astute broker answer these important client questions: What limits of coverage should I buy? What are others paying for these limits? How does my program stack up to theirs? In essence it allows a Consultative Broker® to provide the client with information without forcing him into the marketplace to comparison shop.

Web-based Information Portals

Many clients understand the importance of obtaining quality information quickly. This is particularly true with any firm that must send and receive OSHA data. This type of service allows a broker to brand the information portal under her own name, thereby creating the perception of being the provider of quality information. By providing quality information in a real-time fashion, these brokers make a strong case for reducing a client's administrative overhead and costs.

These are but three examples of specialty resources. As the information age comes faster, more are being created on a regular basis. My experience has shown that the best way to stay current on these is to visit the RIMS annual conference. The showroom floor of RIMS features hundreds of vendors that offer specialty resources to buyers and brokers.

Here are some others:

Additional Specialty Resources

- Forensic Accountants
  – B.I., B&M Claims

- Premium Auditors

- Actuarial Services

- Executive Risk
  – Legal

- Environmental Services

- Regulatory Compliance

- Captive Managers

- Third Party Administrators

The delivery of specialty resources is the most difficult thing for most brokers to do. That is because, for the most part, the deployment of these resources requires a solid understanding of how they can conceptually impact a client's costs. However, once a Consultative Broker® masters these, she will have separated herself from the pack permanently.

Deployment of these resources requires a solid understanding of how they can conceptually impact a client's costs.

Industry Specific Resources

One of the things that successful consultative brokerages do to differentiate themselves is to create *Practice Groups*. This is a strategy that allows them to duplicate resource services and expertise across a geographic boundary. They utilize these practice groups when they are intending to move into a new marketplace or their firm has grown into many offices.

A key ingredient to practice groups, or any resource-based sale, is the deployment of resources geared toward specific industries. Here are a few examples of them:

- Bonding Expertise – Construction Practice Groups

- Clean Room Fire Prevention – High Tech Industry Practice Groups

- Mobile Driver's Training Equipment – Transportation Industry Practice Groups

- JD/RNs (Lawyers with Nursing Degrees) – Healthcare Practice Groups

- Security Experts – Financial Institution Practice Groups

- Crash Site Investigators – Aviation Industry Practice Groups

When a mega-broker calls on an account, the team goes to great lengths to demonstrate each member's abilities inside the prospect's industry. The most important technique is the ability to show the buyer these industry-specific resources. They then make certain that the buyer values these resources and spend the rest of their time showing the prospect how these specific resources will benefit them. In many cases they have already won the competition.

But, let's say that you are an agent/broker that does not have these types of resources on your payroll. You can still arrange for them through third-party vendors. In fact, if you are looking to grow in large accounts, you need to have these types of resource capabilities available to round out your team and to be able to differentiate yourself.

Here is an example of how it would work. You have called on your local municipal aviation authority. While your firm is very familiar with the property issues and even some of the general liability issues, you have never faced some of the specific aviation issues. What do you do?

A Consultative Broker® would then spend time finding who inside North America acts as a wholesaler to that industry. Not for the purposes of simple insurance but to access loss control expertise. In addition, these special wholesalers have London-based connections that greatly expand the local agent/brokers ability to bring innovative risk financing solutions. (These solutions do require a high level of loss control.)

I remember working with a local agent who had an opportunity to work on a large account in the oil and gas industry. This firm had absolutely no expertise inside this complicated industry group. The owner came to me and asked my advice regarding the best way to attract this account. I gave it to him frankly.

"You don't have the qualifications to write this account. While you have an excellent relationship with the CEO, the risk manager and CFO will not work with you unless you find a partner who can provide you this additional expertise," I explained patiently. "If you want to write it, find a wholesaler that specializes in this and feature the wholesaler's loss control services."

"In fact," I told the agent in a hushed voice, "you can take out your toughest mega-broker competition with its own resources. This broker has a resource and wholesale team that specializes in working with regional brokers. This team provides the same high quality resources that the mega-broker uses to compete." I went on to advise, "Get to that team and begin to work on the account with that team as your industry-specialty resource."

Well, you would have thought I had just proposed the Communist Manifesto. This firm was offended that I would recommend bringing in an outsider. But, do you know what the real problem was? The firm didn't want to split the revenue with anyone else!

Here is the classic example of a sales person's ego getting in front of his brain. Truthfully, *a higher percentage of nothing is still nothing*. Without these additional industry-specific resources, this agent was not in a position to bring a client/prospect value.

So, what did the agent do instead? He called on the account and had a meeting that outlined his agency's expertise. Several producers from the firm participated and called themselves experts in the oil and gas arena. They were dismissed after one meeting and the buyer selected the firm that I recommended they work with. The revenue was $180,000. 0% of 0 = 0. 66% of $180,000 = $120,000. Hmmmm . . . a $120,000 ego trip!

As a working Consultative Broker®, the first three new accounts I wrote revolved around the deployment of industry specific resources. In fact, without deploying these industry specific resources, there is little doubt that I would not have been successful.

Here is a quick review of how it happened in each case. Mind you, all of these were accounts based in the Southwest.

Explosive Manufacturer – We worked with an individual in the Northeast who had a strong expertise inside this industry. We wrote the account, even though I had never set foot in an explosives manufacturing firm prior to the first call.

Start-Up Financial Institution – We were appointed the broker based upon our ability to provide one of the top experts inside the financial bonding and executive risk arena. He was based in New York. We wrote the account. I had never read a bankers blanket bond prior to that time.

Major Regional Bus Operator – We obtained this account by bringing in one of the top east coast based transportation wholesalers and loss control providers. We wrote the account, even though I had never previously written a transportation account.

In each case, there was a common denominator: we brought in an industry-specific resource that added value. Frankly, my entire role was to deploy the resource and make certain that the prospect found it to be a valuable addition to the business organization.

Just so you know. Upon being appointed the broker, I did work diligently to understand the issues of the client and did become expert in translating those issues on behalf of the client. They knew my group's value as a gatekeeper of resources that was also technically proficient.

The understanding of how to deploy Specialty and Industry Specific Resources is the final step in the creation of a Consultative Brokerage® value proposition. These resources, in addition to loss control and claims management are the icing on the cake. These are the things that enable a broker to really back up her claim of understanding a client's business.

> *The understanding of how to deploy Specialty and Industry Specific Resources is the final step in the creation of a Consultative Brokerage® value proposition.*

Rob's Rule: Nothing says *"We understand your business"* like specialty and industry-specific resources.

Chapter 17

Institutionalization: The Business-to-Business Approach

"No man is an Island, entire of itself; every man is a piece of the Continent, a part of the main."

John Donne (1572 – 1631)
English clergyman & poet

I nstitutionalization . . . Boy is that a big word! Here is what it means. It is the ability of your firm to be recognized and valued as part of the transaction. When a client understands the culture of your firm and you understand hers, there is a common ground of institutionalization. This transcends the efforts and recognition of individuals. It creates a business-to-business environment.

One of the biggest mistakes an ineffective producer makes is the failure to recognize that business clients want to do business with other businesses. It is very understandable. Most good producers have been tested for high ego drive and the need to win. Because of this, we see it as our responsibility to create the sale and carry it forward solely on our own efforts.

> **One of the biggest mistakes an ineffective producer makes is the failure to recognize that business clients want to do business with other businesses.**

Throughout my brokerage career, I was blessed to interact with some of the finest minds and best people in our industry. One of those people was the late Robert F. Corroon. Bob was the principle of Corroon and Black and a tremendous individual.

As an alumnus of The University of Arizona, Bob made an annual pilgrimage to the Southwest. During several of his trips I was fortunate enough to have some private conversations with him. I once asked him about the keys to production success in the brokerage business. Here was his reply:

"Most of us are highly skilled technicians and excellent salespeople", he responded. "This business is all about creating new relationships. What sets apart the superstars is their ability to create a business relationship with the firm."

> *What sets apart the superstars is their ability to create a business relationship with the firm.*

Wow, what a concept! He then went on to add. "This is still an entrepreneurial business based upon the individual initiatives of producers. However, knowing when to step back and bring in the firm is the key to success."

Hmmmmm . . . Another piece to the puzzle. It took me a while to chew on that, but the answer finally came. If I was to be highly successful, it would be important that I change my sales dialogue. How? By learning to take the spotlight off me and place it on the firm as quickly as possible.

What a revelation. By changing my sales dialogue, I was able to obtain the weight of the firm behind me. I was no longer an individual out in the streets trying to tilt at windmills on my own. This insight alone gave me the confidence to call on larger accounts.

Give me your impression on which of these two sales dialogues sounds more appealing to you:

1. Hi, my name is John Doe. I am one of the top brokers in this marketplace. I handle the insurance programs of some of the largest clients in the area. They deal with me because I know how to obtain the best program possible for them. I am certain that I can do the same for you.

Or

2. Hi, my name is John Doe. I represent XYZ Brokerage Firm. Our organization is one of the top providers of risk financing and cost reduction services in this area. Our clients work with us because our firm knows how to provide them with value. It would be a pleasure to demonstrate to you how we can help you reduce your costs.

Well, what do you think? Obviously, number two is the better way to go. Why? Because it is a message that translates on a business-to-business scale. It takes some of the "rugged individualist" rough edges out of the sales approach. It says to the prospect, "Our firm offers something of value."

The critical message of institutionalization is this . . ."I am not alone. It is in your best interests to speak with me because I represent something much greater than myself."

Here is what the process of institutionalization looks like:

The Process of Institutionalization

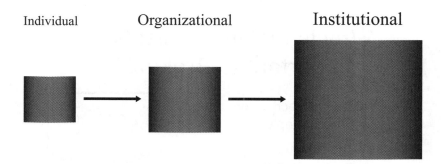

Individual   Organizational   Institutional

As you can see, everything begins with the individual efforts of the producer. Just as Mr. Corroon instructed. Then, as quickly as possible, the organization is introduced into the conversation with the goal of demonstrating the impact of the firm and institutionalization. Successful consultative brokers take the spotlight off themselves as quickly as possible. They see themselves as observers of the process. The main question they ask themselves is this: "Is this buyer valuing our organization"?

Successful consultative brokers take the spotlight off themselves as quickly as possible.

Here are some of the reasons why the ability to institutionalize your organization is very important to the sales process:

1. It takes personalities out of the equation. While building relationships is still important, institutionalization allows buyers to judge how your organization can bring them value. This is especially important when you are competing against a long-term incumbent that has simply sold on personality.

2. It allows you to replicate your story. No matter what type of account you call on, your story will remain the same. You represent an organization that can bring value to the buyer.

3. You can continue to prospect an account over a period of time. As we have already discussed, it usually takes some time to develop a quality prospect. Institutionalization allows you to use the weight of the firm's reputation and advertising efforts to continue to move the prospect firm down the pipeline.

Institutionalization allows you to use the weight of the firm's reputation.

Why Is Institutionalization Important to Brokers?

- Provides protection for production people

- Lets them focus on making business grow

- Provides consistent credibility

- Reinforces relationships

It is important to note that institutionalization is just as important to existing clients as it is to prospects. In fact, I will bet that you have already institutionalized your best existing clients.

Our research has shown that most successful producers and their firms receive a large percentage of revenue from a very small percentage of clients. They get about 40 percent of their income from 5 percent of their clients. Therefore, a successful producer who handles 70 accounts totaling $600,000 of income will probably find the following to be true: Three to five clients will yield around $240,000 of income.

Whenever I speak to a group of brokers I ask them to note their top five clients as we focus on our workshop. Invariably, they have little trouble identifying who those top five are. Likewise, a firm who has 1,000 commercial accounts totaling $10 million in revenue will find that about fifty of these top *Franchise Accounts* bringing them $4 million in revenue.

Here is a universal truth: The top 5 percent of your accounts are funding virtually all your success. These are the ones that are critical to your income as a producer. Imagine what a bad day it becomes when (or if) you lose one. Successful consultative brokers know this and make certain they wrap the resources of the firm around these clients. They focus on having the client become wedded to their organizations and take care that all members of their brokerages know the importance of these *Franchise Accounts*.

Who are your *Franchise Accounts*? What have you done to institutionalize these accounts? Are they under attack by other firms? What would happen to your revenue stream if one of these accounts were to leave you?

Those are some tough questions that need to be asked. As I always say, it is better to ask the tough questions of yourselves now, rather than later after the revenue is gone. It is less expensive too!

These are the Consultative Brokerage® steps that lead to institutionalization of a firm's *Franchise Accounts*.

Steps in *Franchise Account* Institutionalization

Individual	Organizational	Institutional
Individual acts by producers, designed to create opportunities for the organization.	Resources of the firm are deployed in support of the individual.	The relationship becomes part of the firm culture. A partnership is established.

Whether it is a new prospect, or an existing franchise account, Institutionalization provides a platform of value. As the following chapter will illustrate, it does need to be created and nurtured. All members of your firm must walk like they talk and understand its importance.

Rob's Rule: You will either create your firm's culture or *inherit* one. If you create it, you can choose what it will be!

Chapter 18

Techniques of Institutionalization

"In preparing for battle I have always found that plans are useless, but planning is indispensable."

Dwight D. Eisenhower
34th president of US 1953 – 1961 (1890 – 1969)

A common misconception frequently arises when an organization institutionalizes an account in a clumsy manner. In such cases, producers rightfully see the firm as intruding upon their entrepreneurial spirit. But, thankfully, in most cases institutionalization is used to help the producer move a prospect down the pipeline or continue to secure the renewal rights to a client.

Throughout my career I saw institutionalization attempted for the wrong reasons only once. This was in a situation with an extremely weak sales leader who wanted to incorporate a contact relations management system in order to spy on producers. His notion was that he could then look at their calendars and see who was actually working on new accounts. I reminded him that a better way to determine who was working on new accounts was to look at their new business production numbers! By the way, his concept failed after he had spent $10,000 in program costs as all his producers revolted.

Institutionalization should never be used to control sales people or make all things equal. One of the universal truths of a sales organization is the existence of a hierarchy in every firm. The producers who create the most revenue in a profitable manner are at the top of the food chain. Also, institutionalization does not take the place of a producer's responsibility to maintain and grow their relationships. It is an aid, not a replacement.

Institutionalization
Is Not!

- A Method of Controlling Individual Production Effort

- A Substitute for Relationships

- An Excuse for Not Following up Individually

- Socialism/Communism

So, let's talk for a few minutes about how successful firms and producers work hand in hand to create institutionalization.

Prospect Lists

It blows me away to see how few firms actually have quality prospect lists. I suppose this is a throwback to the rugged individualist days. But, here is the problem: unless you have a quality prospect list, your firm can never help a producer gain ground. When that is the case, every activity relies entirely on the producer's sole efforts and the strengths of your organization are not leveraged.

A firm-wide prospect list allows the organization to help the producer carry the ball. Throughout the course of the prospecting cycle the firm can include this prospect in all of its marketing efforts. Whether they are mailings, invitations to events, or announcements, it allows the producers to focus on additional efforts as the firm helps them create a business-to-business relationship.

A firm-wide prospect list allows the organization to help the producer carry the ball.

Some producers will resist the inclusion of their deals on a prospect list. When this occurs it is usually driven by one or two reasons. Either they don't have any prospects or they don't trust their own organization. In each of these cases, there are other issues that need to be addressed!

Here is the bottom line in today's world of business. It is imperative that the firm have a good handle on their top prospects. Not to control producers, but to help them. Once a firm and broker embark on Consultative Brokerage®, they need to include their prospects in this discussion.

Here is a short true story. I was in a major southeastern city leading a TCOR workshop for a relatively large independent agency. At one point I asked for group members to share information on several of their large prospects so that I could give examples of how to approach these clients.

I stood there for several seconds and nobody responded. So I asked again. Still no response from anyone in the audience. At that point, I thought it best to take a little break as perhaps they needed a short rest. Maybe I had just worn them out.

During the break, one of the producers approached me and told me in a hushed voice, "Rob, you just don't understand our firm." He went on to add, "The reason nobody is talking about prospects is because we all see each other as competitors. If I talk about a prospect, someone else in the room will find out I am working on what he believes is his prospect."

"WHAT!?! Are you kiddin' me, Laddie? Do you mean to tell me that each of you sees the other as the enemy?" Apparently so.

Well, I decided to hang in there and get one of them to talk. I finally coerced someone to give me some of the details of a prospect, including the name. What do you think happened? A guy across the room started filling in the blanks regarding additional information on this prospect. Then another guy began providing more background. By the time we were done, the initial producer had more insight than he ever could have gained working by himself.

So, before I left, this group got one of my best hellfire and brimstone speeches. Mussolini from the balcony had nothing on me. I told them in no uncertain terms that unless they started sharing information and institutionalizing their accounts, they could soon expect to have no pipeline whatsoever. Ah, that was a good day!

Office Visits

One of the best tactics that the mega-brokers use is the office visit. They understand that if a prospect visits their offices, they have broken down some of the barriers. During this visit, the prospect (or client) is introduced to a number of people who are involved with the firm.

They understand that if a prospect visits their offices, they have broken down some of the barriers.

Now to be honest, touring an insurance brokerage is about as interesting as watching paint dry. Cubicle after cubicle, with a number of computer terminals, and the offices along the windows for the executives, managers, and key producers. Soooooo interesting.

But, that is not the point. Here are the facts. Just the very action of a prospect being there should tell you a lot. They are seriously considering a business relationship with your organization. This is the best chance they will ever get to kick the tires before the deal is done. So, here are a few tips regarding institutionalization of your firm during an office visit by a prospect. They may seem obvious to you, but believe me, I have seen the opposite done on several occasions.

1. Make certain that all members of your firm know they are coming and who they are. There is nothing worse than groups of employees gathered together wondering and staring at these "new" people in the office.

2. Do not allow the visit to occur on casual day if your casual day gives employees the chance to wear tattered blue jeans and Grateful Dead tee shirts. (Casual day and slob day are two different things!)

3. Clean up your conference room and spend some money on it. Just because the board table was first purchased seventy-five years ago by the firm's founder doesn't make it presentable. If it looks like a seventy-five-year-old table it says, "Hey, we would like to afford better and maybe we can if you give us your business."

Tell the Same Story

It is imperative that all members of your firm tell the same story whenever they are in contact with the public. Why? Because in many cases a prospect that one producer is working with may run into another firm member at any number of functions (chamber meetings, trade groups, public service, etc.). If each of these firm members tells a different story regarding the focus of your firm, institutionalization will be destroyed.

If each of these firm members tells a different story regarding the focus of your firm, institutionalization will be destroyed.

As a working broker, I had spent about a year gaining the trust of a high level networking group. I had consistently presented our firm as a "risk financing and cost reduction organization." I had patiently spent time creating the awareness that our firm possessed resources and capabilities that our clients used to reduce their Total Cost of Risk.

Well, one night I took an eager young producer with me to this monthly networking meeting. As we sat around the dinner table of eight the time came for each of us to introduce ourselves and our firm. Junior introduced himself first and proudly announced, "We are an insurance agency and we sell insurance to businesses. We represent a number of insurance companies and can usually save our customers money by reducing their premiums."

In two sentences and ten seconds he undid what it had taken me one year to accomplish. Needless to say, I then spent the rest of the evening in damage control. Oh, and by the way, I never brought Junior to another meeting!

The process of institutionalization is one of the most important initiatives a firm must focus on. It allows the producer to really supercharge production by utilizing the weight of the organization. Also, it allows the firm to truly choose what its business reputation will be.

Rob's Rule: There is an "I" in team. What it stands for is institutionalization!

Chapter 19

Broker Control: The Final Touch

"Do it now. It is not safe to leave a generous feeling to the cooling influences of the world."

Thomas Guthrie, 1803–1873 Scottish Divine and philanthropist

B roker Control is inevitable in every transaction. Someone always has it. Either you, your competitor, or, in some cases, your prospect always gets it at some point. You know what I mean.

Have you ever felt that you were on the outside "looking in" when working on a new account? You have thrown all your best stuff at the prospect and you still feel like you are standing on shifting sands. No matter what you do, you just can't seem to get a feel for the outcome.

Why does this occur? Because someone else has broker control. This individual will get the last look, will be the one who get the markets, and may even be the person who helps the prospect "review your proposal." Someone always has it.

As a Consultative Broker® it is critical that you know where you stand. It is vital that you obtain broker control before you make your presentation. Without this, your presentation will fall on deaf ears or at worst; it will be passed on to your competitors. The entire Consultative Brokerage® process is about obtaining, keeping, and validating your broker control.

> **The entire Consultative Brokerage® process is about obtaining, keeping, and validating your broker control.**

Here are just a few of the reasons why you must determine your level of broker control.

- Your team depends upon you for guidance on the next move. You have deployed several people as resources and they look to you as their leader.

- It allows you to predict an outcome. The Consultative Brokerage® Process is based upon establishing a value proposition. You need a yardstick by which to measure your success.

- It validates the expense of the Consultative Brokerage® Methodology. Consultative Brokerage® is more intricate than simply providing quotes and involves several moving parts. You need to know where you stand.

- If you don't obtain broker control, someone else will. After all, as we mentioned earlier, someone always has it.

Why Must Broker Control Be Established?

- Your Team Depends Upon It

- Allows Prediction of Outcome

- Validates Expense of Consultative Process

- If You Don't, Somebody Else Will

A seasoned broker can actually feel it happening. This is the culmination of the Consultative Brokerage® Methodology. Everything has led up to the point of broker control changing hands.

Now that you have identified the issues, built all the right relationships, provided resources to address issues, and confirmed the client understanding of your firm's value, there is but one thing left to do. Prove it in a Total Cost of Risk Presentation and request the client appoint you as the broker. Simple enough, eh?

Establishing broker control is the equivalent of *setting the hook*. You have waited patiently on the prospect pond. You have skillfully presented the tasty morsels of quality, TCOR, and value. Your prospect has nibbled at the succulent taste of cost reduction. Your firm has established its platform and now is the time.

Yank the rod! Now you either have broker control or you don't. It will never get better than this. You have done all the right things. You have earned the right to ask the prospect for his or her business. Don't wait any longer.

Broker Control, the Final Touch

- The Prospects - Selected and Matured with Issues
- The Relationships - Depth and Strength
- The Resources - Deployed and Valued
- The Firm - Institutionalized and Consistent

Broker Control Is the Difference!

This is the moment that everything has led up to. The Consultative Brokerage® Methodology has provided you with a roadmap. Now, you only need to confirm whether or not you have broker control. If you don't have it, you must keep your powder dry and not go forward into the presentation. Somewhere along the line you have missed a step. Or, you have been working with a bad prospect!

If you don't have it, you must keep your powder dry and not go forward into the presentation.

So, how do you confirm whether or not you have broker control? A seasoned Consultative Broker® knows that the answer lies in the previous four principles of Consultative Brokerage®. She uses the Consultative Brokerage® Methodology to judge her progress and client acceptance. It tells her exactly when to set the hook. If the previous four principles are in place, she knows the meal is ready to be served. She then moves on to the Broker of Record appointment process.

How do you ask for the Broker of Record letter? By making a presentation based upon your TCOR findings. This presentation takes the form of a consulting presentation that lays out the facts in a conceptual fashion. If it is a presentation to a prospect, it is a *conceptual* presentation showing the prospect how you will provide value and reduce costs. If it is a current account, this is done through a stewardship report.

The final two sections of this book will show you some of the basics of TCOR and how to make quality presentations. These last two Consultative Brokerage® techniques are the culmination of successfully orchestrating the Five Principles of Consultative Brokerage®. You know the issues; the client knows your firm and you have marshaled the resources that will allow you to make a TCOR presentation. In fact, the prospect is now anxiously awaiting your presentation because he knows you are really going to help his company obtain what he wants. Better performance on the balance sheet.

So, we will now go further.

Rob's Rule: If you don't establish broker control, someone else will!

Chapter 20

Understanding Total Cost of Risk

"Customers pay only for what is of use to them and gives them value. Nothing else constitutes quality."

Peter Drucker (1909 – 2005)
Author

WARNING: Skipping right to TCOR will be hazardous to your Consultative Brokerage® development. The principles of Consultative Brokerage® must be followed before attempting a TCOR presentation. Failure to do so will lead to low probability of success.

T he term Total Cost of Risk was first introduced into the risk management community in 1962. Frankly, I wish we could take credit for it, but rather than try and come up with a catchy name, we decided to stay with the industry acronym of TCOR. Our role is to help you as working brokers and carriers understand how to apply these concepts, not pretend to invent them!

You may be surprised to learn that sophisticated risk managers have the same problem that you do. They must always justify their budget and costs to their CFOs. So, in an effort to show their bosses the effective return on their investment, the term Total Cost of Risk was born.

In this sense, TCOR gives the ultimate buyer (budget approver) a yardstick by which to measure the effectiveness of the risk management program. This places the risk management process on a return on investment platform rather than simply letting it be seen as an expense.

In its purest sense the risk management TCOR process was designed to judge the effectiveness of risk in three areas: property, tort liability, and occupational disease or injury.

For purposes of Consultative Brokerage® we have made some subtle changes to the initial Total Cost of Risk concepts. They are:

- The original TCOR was designed primarily for large self-insured firms. Consultative Brokerage® has adapted this concept for the middle market buyer, which in many cases stays in the traditional marketplace.

- We place a great emphasis on the *indirect* loss costs rather than on the direct. In many cases the middle market buyer transfers the direct loss to carriers but must retain the indirect loss costs.

- We believe that any resource you as a broker provide the client is a reduction in administrative costs. Without these services, the client would have to purchase them elsewhere in order to obtain the return on investment.

- Rather than simply the property, casualty, and worker's compensation, our version of the TCOR concept touches on the client's entire enterprise risk. Therefore a Consultative Broker® is able to demonstrate her impact across the client's entire business model.

The Consultative Brokerage® TCOR model encompasses four areas of client costs. They are as follows: Insurance Premiums, Loss Costs (direct and indirect), Administration Costs, and lastly Premium Taxes or Fees.

Total Cost of Risk Components

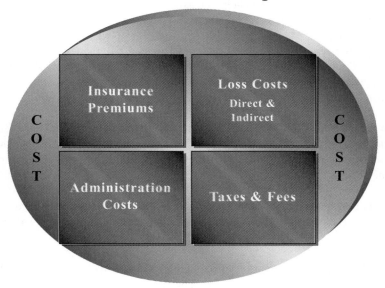

As a Consultative Broker® we must first understand the holistic approach of TCOR. In the event any one of these components expands or contracts the entire cost of risk is affected accordingly. They are not separate entities but merely one component that impacts the total.

Why is this important? Because it coincides with what we already know. In many cases a client's premium cost is the smallest part of the company's costs. By showing this *holistically* (boy I like that word) we are able to keep things in perspective and represent premium costs for what they are . . . a small part of the whole.

Also, for those of you are practicing Consultative Brokerage® and competing against someone who isn't, it places you in a competitive advantage. A Consultative Broker® will be able to demonstrate an impact in the other areas that outshine someone that is simply competing on the commodity.

We will talk more about this in upcoming chapters, but for now simply ask yourself these questions:

1. In a hard market, with premiums increasing, what would the client's reaction be if you could show her how you have actually *reduced* her costs?

2. In a soft market, with your competition selling price, would a client be willing to pay you more in premium if she knew your costs were less expensive?

I think you know the answers to those questions. If not, I've got some swamp land in Florida I would like to sell you!

That is the point of the TCOR value proposition. You can focus your sales and service strategy on an outcome that benefits your clients and prospects. It allows you to compete at a higher level no matter what your competition, or in some cases carriers, does in the arena of price. It just doesn't matter!

> *You can focus your sales and service strategy on an outcome that benefits your clients and prospects.*

It makes me crazy to see how many agents lose their minds when a new hot carrier comes into their marketplace. Suddenly, obtaining this carrier *du jour* becomes the entire focus of the agency or agent. Whenever the producer loses an account it is because he just didn't have this right carrier. Or, he lives in fear that another agent will call on his client and "get" this carrier.

Here is a universal truth about the agency/brokerage business. Once you start chasing every hot carrier, you have taken the focus away from the important issue . . . reducing your client's costs. Here are some other universal truths. In a softening marketplace you will need to attract a different carrier weekly to keep the cheapest price. In a hardening marketplace you will spend all your time begging!

> *Once you start chasing every hot carrier, you have taken the focus away from the important issue . . . reducing your client's costs.*

But, here is what consultative brokers know. Hard or soft markets don't matter. That is simply what the insurance marketplace offers. The lion's share of client costs are controlled by these astute brokers.

I think it has been summed up best by the chairman of one of our top brokerage clients. He has consistently instructed his brokers on this point: "Make certain that all of our clients know that when the premiums rise, not to blame us. Also, make certain that they know when the premiums fall not to give us the credit." He then makes the following keen observation, "Don't take the blame or credit because we didn't do it."

So, what is this brokerage executive referring to? The fact that the marketplace is generally outside your control. But, when a Consultative Broker® works inside the TCOR process, she is able to keep the light shining where it should be: On her impact!

Rob's Rule: Keep the TCOR light shining on your client value and impact.

Chapter 21

Insurance and Fees: The Least Important TCOR Components

"Never again clutter your days or nights with so many menial and unimportant things that you have no time to accept a real challenge when it comes along."

Og Mandino (1923 – 1996)
Author

I t is important that you understand the interaction of the four components of Total Cost of Risk. This is not intended to be a dry lecture, but rather a discussion of how these TCOR components become a living, breathing entity. Living and breathing because they will assist you in feeding your family!

As a working broker who followed this mantra, I can tell you that it was exciting to find ways to reduce a prospect's costs by using TCOR. In this process, you become a detective searching for the clues that all the other brokers have passed over. Once you discover these clues, it is simply a matter of proving your hypothesis. TCOR provides you the vehicle of proof.

> *You become a detective searching for the clues that all the other brokers have passed over.*

In this chapter we will discuss the two components that you have the least control over. Let's get these out of the way so that we can get to the meat of the sandwich.

Insurance/Risk Financing

In most middle market accounts, the risk financing vehicle is insurance. While some will utilize a high deductible or retrospective rating program, our focus is primarily on standard insurance programs. Frankly, if more sophisticated vehicles are used, the TCOR methodology only gets better because of pure loss dollars. But, we will save this discussion for another time.

TCOR Component
Insurance Costs

- Cost to Transfer the Risk
  - Insurance premiums

- Must Be to Third Party
  - Not a fully self-insured layer

- Type of Program Is Important
  - Loss sensitive versus first dollar

- Vital Assumption
  - All insurance costs will change in the future

This first component of TCOR is very straightforward. It is the premium. Now mind you that for today, we are *not* talking about highly sophisticated risk transfer mechanisms. Therefore there are some rules that we must be keep in mind:

1. This component consists primarily of the premium or cost of the risk transfer. Any costs that are absorbed by the client in the area of high deductibles or retained loss must be accounted for in the loss cost component. Therefore, this component is the pure premium and must be paid to a third party.

2. All premiums will change in the future depending upon losses and the underwriting marketplace. (Hold this thought until we get to the subject of benchmarking.)

So, the premium is the premium. It is as simple as that. Hard market or soft market, it doesn't matter. So, we won't spend any more time on this subject except to tell you a little story.

> *So, the premium is the premium. It is as simple as that.*

When I first started our consulting and training firm I was invited to address a smaller agency in a west coast city. As I have previously mentioned, I can usually tell who the Doubting Thomas is in the audience, and this was no exception. At the end of the conference table sat a salty dog with his hands clasped behind his neck. I just wasn't getting through to him.

After the mid-morning break this individual returned a changed man. He was so excited he just couldn't wait to tell the group. "It works", he proudly announced and then repeated again to make sure all knew. "It works!"

Now, I wasn't expecting this response from him because I believed he was a lost cause. To be honest, I was afraid he was talking about bathroom fixtures so I asked him to expand on his exclamation.

"I just got off the phone with an underwriter", he explained. "We have been negotiating a cost reduction on one of my clients. I told her I needed the premium to be $135,000 and she said her company needed $160,000."

At this point I started to cringe until he finished his story. "So I told her," he went on proudly, "I don't have time to argue with you, I am here at a seminar on Consultative Brokerage® and need to get back."

Well, as my former Doubting Thomas tells it, the underwriter stopped him in mid sentence and said "Hold on, are you really at a seminar on how to be consultative? If that is the case, we are looking for agents who understand that approach. So, I will get you the premium you need."

If you have stayed with me this long, I think you can tell that getting premium reductions from underwriters is not the **key** strategy of Consultative Brokerage®. But, in this case, I allowed the broker to give me credit for this miracle. Hey, sometimes you got to take it when it comes!

Taxes & Fees

These are simply a function of the insurance premiums. If the premium changes, they do. As an aside, some of you may know that high-deductible programs were created for primarily one reason, to escape premium taxes. The losses inside the deductible layer originally were not taxed by regulators as premiums, although some jurisdictions have taken steps to change this. Therefore, the original concept was to reduce the cost of the program accordingly. These schemes (that's a term the Brits use at Lloyds) have been also transferred to help underwriters during a hard market.

TCOR Component
Taxes & Fees

- State Insurance Taxes
- Self-Insured Bonds
- Letters of Credit
- Self-Insured Retentions

So, the Taxes and Fees are something over which you as a broker have very little control. They are simply an attendant cost of the premium. The regulators determine these, and most of the time they are invisible to you and your client unless you are in a self-insured or non-admitted program.

In keeping with our well established motto of "The Premium is the Premium," we won't spend any more time on this subject. Perhaps in a future book we will talk about the keys of successful broking and how to effectively utilize cash flow and underwriter negotiations. But, not today!

Rob's Rule: Let the other brokers fight over the premium. Spend your time where you can really make a difference!

Chapter 22

Loss and Administrative Costs: The Meat of the TCOR Sandwich

"All truths are easy to understand once they are discovered; the point is to discover them."

Galileo Galilei
Italian astronomer & physicist (1564 – 1642)

H

ere it is Ladies and Gentlemen. The moment you have been waiting for. If you have stayed with me this long you are ready to take the big step. THE BIGGIE. This is the piece that will change your thinking forever. It is the icing on the cake, the meat of the sandwich, and the *Coup de grace*.

Remember our previous discussion of resource capabilities and how a Consultative Broker® deploys them to reduce client costs? If not, go back to chapters 13, 14, and 15.

Do you know what the entire reason for this deployment is? Why, to reduce a client's loss costs and administrative costs of course. Once they can show a client how they do that, the rest is child's play. It allows them to mutter those magic words. Oh, and by the way, we offer insurance policies too! (See Chapter 9.)

The Four Quadrants of Resources are designed with two things in mind: to reduce loss and administrative costs. It is through the application of these resources that a skilled Consultative Broker® fulfills his role as a detective. Consultative brokers are always asking themselves this question: How can our firm reduce this client's losses and business overhead?

Loss Cost and Indirect Loss Costs

Again, place firmly in your mind one of the most important concepts you will ever learn. Even a buyer of first dollar insurance programs has a huge business cost tied up in indirect loss costs. This is the lost economic impact, the lost opportunity cost, or the lost productivity. These are the loss costs you are attacking.

So, as you apply your resources and reduce the loss costs, you are also reducing the indirect loss costs as well. In some cases, these indirect costs are larger than the claim itself. Remember we are now talking about a client's business model.

While all of this is happening, what is really taking place? The client's TCOR is also dropping. That is why a premium can actually go up and yet the TCOR can go down. But, it is up to you to explain and quantify it in a TCOR calculation. Remember, quantification is the key. Anything less is simply a list of features.

TCOR Component
Loss Costs

Loss Costs
Direct &
Indirect

- ## Two Primary Types of Direct Losses
  – Retained and Loss-Sensitive Programs

- ## Business Opportunity Loss
  – People, Places, and Things

- ## Resource Impact
  – Push/Pull of Claims and Loss Control

- ## Impact Must Be Quantifiable
  – Anything less is just a *feature!*

In the event your prospect or client has a program that retains losses (i.e., self-retained or loss sensitive) the TCOR calculation really sings. In this case, your client gets the benefit directly of your assistance in loss cost reduction.

However, in many middle and upper middle market accounts, the direct loss costs are transferred to the carrier. So, when you apply the quadrants of resources, you need to show how they improve a prospect's or client's business opportunities. How can we improve their financial statements?

Also, keep in mind the Push/Pull Impact of claims and loss control. These two quadrants of resources are interdependent and, when combined, they supercharge the client impact. This is not to mention that they provide you an exit barrier that will last well into the future! (The continued ability to guarantee an outcome.)

Lastly, don't forget our old friend quantification. The application of the resources along with your corresponding loss reduction is the outcome. Make it real.

When you show a prospect your potential to reduce his company's TCOR, you are talking about how your resources will be applied to current and future losses. You are placing a value on each of these losses and showing the prospect how much they are costing. Then you are showing how to reduce or remove them with your resources and what this will mean in improved profitability.

Administration Cost Reduction

The reduction of administrative cost revolves entirely around your ability to provide specialty and industry specific resources. The application of these resources allows a Consultative Broker® the ability to help prospects reduce costs that are already on their balance sheets through improved efficiency.

TCOR Component
Administration Cost

- ### Staff Personnel
  – Clerical and Safety

- ### Implementation and Monitoring Expenses
  – Time and Money

- ### Outside Services
  – Pre-Loss and Post-Loss

  – Reports and Inspections

If we can provide a prospect improved efficiencies through quick information, less time utilized in program administration, or specialized training, we have reduced their costs. Also, if we bring in preloss or postloss services that they would have paid for, we have also reduced their costs.

Here are some examples of how administrative costs are reduced by your resources:

Resource	Application	Quantified Value
Specialized Safety Training	Provides efficiency, rather than the client trying to create it.	The cost to the client of development and time spent in delivering the material.
Internet Information Portal	Provides the client with information that reduces time in research.	The cost of employees spending time on gathering research.
Loss Control Studies (i.e. ergonomic, pollution, etc)	Provides client specialized reports as part of the relationship or at a reduced cost because of the relationship.	The cost of obtaining these studies in the event a third party vendor was engaged.

It always amazes me how many resources and projects are committed to a client without any thought of the value the client or prospect will receive. We place that under the heading of, "We just do it." A simple example is that of a contractor who has a certificate of insurance program that is all balled up. As part of your service, you help the client untie the knot of several hundred pieces of paper. What is that worth? How much money did the client spend on internal administration that you removed? Take the credit. Lord knows we have enough chances to get blamed for the bad stuff!

Here is one of the caveats of TCOR. The only way to impact loss costs and administrative costs is through the application of resources. While it is true that the risk financing costs and taxes are impacted by resources through a potential reduction in premium, the purest and quickest reduction in client costs are delivered solely by your ability to apply resources.

The TCOR Adjustment Formula

Cost of Risk Financing + Resources Impact = TCOR Adjustment

Risk Financing ——————→ Insurance$ and Resources Impact

Loss Costs ——————→ Resources Impact

Administrative Costs ——→ Resources Impact

Taxes and Fees ——————→ Insurance$ and Resources Impact

50% of TCOR Factors Are Not about the Insurance!

So, now we have the formula and a clearer understanding of how TCOR fits with the resources of a Consultative Brokerage®. We should also be coming to a conclusion about why a Total Cost of Risk value proposition is so powerful. It is tailored to each client and specific business. It answers the prospect's question, "What makes you unique"?

Rob's Rule: Loss costs and administrative costs are where the TCOR action is.

Chapter 23

The Application of Loss and Administrative Cost Reduction

"The important thing is not to stop questioning."

Albert Einstein
US (German-born) physicist (1879 – 1955)

There is no manual that shows a broker exactly what the indirect cost of loss actually is. Also, the application of your resources to reduce administrative costs is not in the manual either. To understand these costs it is important to have a discussion with your prospects or clients in order to understand their business models.

> *It is important to have a discussion with your prospects or clients in order to understand their business models.*

I am often asked, "How do I determine a client's costs?" Well, after a great deal of thought, I usually reply, "ASK THEM!" Deep, eh?

I was recently holding a day-long seminar for one of our private clients. As part of the event the client had invited three of his clients to be part of a panel discussion. I began the session by asking each panelist what his biggest business challenge was. Notice I said *business* challenge, not insurance challenge. The answers I received were fascinating.

One gentleman was the CFO of a private jet renovation company. His firm rebuilt older model private jets and modernized them. Because of this, the company could present a jet into the market in a short time frame. If a buyer ordered a new one there was a three to four year wait. His biggest challenge was finding ways to reduce the timeframe of introduction as this was the company's competitive advantage.

Another panelist represented one of the largest book and magazine distributors in North America. His biggest challenge was doing business in a marketplace that had very little growth. Whenever you find this situation it usually translates to another issue . . . very small margins. In this buyer's case the margin was about 2 percent.

The third participant had a challenge I never anticipated. His business was manufacturing and distributing marble countertops. His biggest challenge was instilling a customer service culture in a business that was manufacturing and contractor driven. He wanted to build a brand based upon customer service excellence.

If I had been a working broker I would have had the answers I needed. As I might have mentioned to you, a working Consultative Broker® has a rolodex spinning in her mind constantly when interviewing a new prospect. What resources can we bring to bear that will help this prospect impact his company's business model?

A working Consultative Broker® has a rolodex spinning in her mind constantly when interviewing a new prospect.

So, hypothetically speaking, here would be my next action items in the attraction of these prospects:

Aviation Account—Set up a loss control visit for a tour of the facilities. Instruct the loss control expert to identify any issues that could delay production or create a bottleneck. In conjunction with loss control, demonstrate to the prospect how we would remove these obstacles and help the company decrease production time. Translate this to productivity and improved profits.

Magazine Distributor—With a 2 percent profit margin we know that every dollar by which we reduce costs is multiplied fifty times in top line revenue (100% / 2% = 50). The buyer has a seven figure workers compensation expense. Obtain loss data and true loss control program information. Demonstrate to the buyer ways to reduce indirect loss costs. For every dollar we reduce loss costs, there is a corresponding indirect loss cost according to OSHA. Demonstrate this impact through the push/pull of claims and loss control. Quantify it and translate it to the buyer's financials.

Marble Countertop Manufacturer—This buyer is astute enough to realize that his brand image is a critical part of his firm's success. He has invested a great deal of time and money to educate and train his employees on the people skills required to be successful. Also, he is particularly concerned about his customer's satisfaction in case a loss or damage is caused by his firm. Demonstrate to this buyer ways that we can reduce his costs through the application of an information portal that will provide high quality training material, loss prevention, and claims reporting. Show the buyer how this will align itself with his business model.

Now, I don't profess to be an expert in any of these businesses. But, I am in mine. So, by asking for business challenges I can reach into the mind of the buyer and identify issues that are outside the standard definition of insurance risk. Then it is merely a matter of bringing in our specific resources and showing the client how we can either reduce his costs or contribute to the success of his business.

So, here are the approaches an astute Consultative Broker® would follow:

Prospect	Issue	Resource	Impact
Private Jet Rebuilder	Competitive Advantage of Time	Loss control program to identify and remove potential friction in manufacturing.	Speed up delivery time-frames. Quantify ability to create additional percentage of revenues by adding to percentage of capacity.
Magazine Distributor	Flat sales at a low profit of 2 percent.	Apply all four quadrants in order to create workers compensation cost reduction. Attack reserves, improve loss control and improve delivery of information to prospect.	Aside from the obvious of reducing insurance costs, the prospect's indirect loss costs and administrative costs will be reduced. For every $1 of loss costs we reduce or avoid, the prospect receives the top-line benefit of 50 times this impact.
Marble Countertop Manufacturer	Improve client service and brand	Provide employee training by using information portal and reduce problems on client jobsites by training, investigation, and reporting.	Build a quality assurance program based upon the resources provided. This greatly reduces the administrative costs of the client. Quantify the value of this program if provided by a third party, and track the effectiveness in customer satisfaction and reduced claim costs.

As you can see, each of the above value propositions revolves around the ability to provide resources and demonstrate the impact to the client. This is the stumbling block of most brokers as they usually skip the steps of "client challenges" and go straight to the insurance program. When this happens, they usually don't get what they want, because they forgot to focus on what the client wanted . . . a more efficient business model.

Do you remember our earlier conversation on what CFOs focus on inside the Enterprise Risk model? Hasn't each one of these issues been tied to increased profitability? Now you are cookin' with gas, and your ability to impact costs through resources is the flame!

Rob's Rule: Ask prospects for the answers to the test, listen closely, and find a way to help them get what they want.

Chapter 24

Moving to a Client Balance Sheet

"The truth is in the eyes
Cause the eyes don't lie, amen"

"Smiling Faces Sometimes," by The Undisputed Truth
– 1971 Popular Song

So now we have it all together. You understand Consultative Brokerage® and how to work with the five principles. You know where to seek resources inside the Four Quadrants. You have a basic understanding of Total Cost of Risk. But, we haven't talked about the missing piece. This is the one that brings it all into focus and allows you to work with a financial buyer on her company's balance sheet. In order to do this we must have a method of quantifiable measurement.

So, before we leave this section, we need to talk about benchmarking and how a Consultative Broker® uses it to demonstrate quantifiable results. In order to create value, there are two very important issues that must be determined.

- The unit of measurement that will be used (rate).

- The time frame that will be compared. (benchmark and comparison period).

Any consultant will tell you that in order to show value, there must be a unit to benchmark results against. This unit of measurement is usually a revenue or expense ratio from a period of time in the past. What measure do most agents and brokers use to compare themselves against? Why, last year's premium of course!

What! Do you mean to say that your only unit of measurement is the most recent premium? Wow, what a difficult business you must be in. Having to earn your spurs every year based solely upon last year must wear you out. Some years, especially if nothing spectacular happened, it must be difficult to really show what your value was.

This is precisely the reason why consultative brokers know that they must use a very different method of demonstrating their impact and results. This method must stand the test of value and be capable of crossing time boundaries that well exceed one year.

As you know, whenever CFOs look at their income and expense statement they use a ratio of each expense line item against sales. That is the true test of their success or failure in impacting profits. They create a rate per one thousand dollars of sales. This rate per thousand is used to compare one period to another as revenues change. It is the only accurate measure of business costs as revenues fluctuate.

So, as consultative brokers, we understand that it is imperative to translate any change of costs to a rate per thousand dollars of sales. This allows us the ability to quantify and demonstrate the impact in a businesslike fashion. This keeps the focus on the ultimate cost rather than simply the price in a changing marketplace.

Therefore, they establish a benchmark date and a comparison period.

There is one other issue of which you should be aware. This is the concept of *comparison period*. Every quality consulting group uses a comparison period of some type in order to judge its results. Therefore, they establish a benchmark date and a comparison period. In many cases, the comparison period will span several years. The common unit of measurement (rate per $1k of revenues) allows you to do this with credibility. While premiums and losses will fluctuate from year to year, the rate per $1k of sales brings it all into proper focus.

In keeping with our tradition of a brief example for the purposes of *this* book, here is what I mean. Recently, one of our clients called on a manufacturer of storage containers. The buyer indicated that the company had been with its workers compensation broker for a number of years and were *"well taken care of."* This opinion was based on the fact that premiums had declined each of the previous two years.

A Consultative Broker® knows that things are not always as they seem if premium is the benchmark. So, our intrepid broker asked for the past three years of loss data, the *true* loss control program, and a financial statement. Here is what he discovered:

A Consultative Broker® knows that things are not always as they seem if premium is the benchmark.

A. The losses had increased each year.

B. The broker had not provided any assistance in the implementation of a loss control program or claims management.

C. The profit margin of the buyer was 5 percent.

So, in order to provide the buyer with a true assessment of the company's Total Cost of Risk, the broker used information from the company to determine that

1. The losses for each year should be multiplied by an indirect loss cost factor of $1.25.

2. The Total Cost of Risk was a combination of premium plus the indirect loss costs.

3. The Benchmark Period should be results from three years ago.

4. The Comparison Period should be the combined results of the past two years.

5. The rate per $1k of revenue is determined by dividing the TCOR by revenues per $1k (i.e. $1,098,750/$59,500 = $18.47).

6. The TCOR expense increase is determined by multiplying the rate difference by the revenues during the comparison period ($1.29 X $59,500).

7. The amount of sales needed to cover the increased TCOR is determined by dividing the TCOR expense by the profit margin ($76,811/.05).

| | Benchmark Period | | Comparison Period | |
	3 Years Ago	2 Years Ago	Last Year	Past 2 Years
Premium	437,000	385,000	345,000	730,000
Revenues	28,500,000	28,500,000	31,000,000	59,500,000
Losses	42,000	110,000	185,000	295,000
Indirect Loss Costs	52,500	137,500	231,250	368,750
Total Cost of Risk	489,500	522,500	576,250	1,098,750
TCOR Rate Per $1k	17.18	18.33	18.59	18.47
Difference in TCOR Rate Per $1k			1.29	
TCOR Expense Increase			76,811	
Sales Needed to Cover Increased TCOR Expenses			1,536,228	

WELL NOW! What do we have here? This looks like a case of a broker simply selling the client insurance and taking credit for the decrease in premium. Remember, the client indicated that the company was being *"well taken care of."* It was being taken care of all right. I call this prospect Corrigan Container for a reason. They were going the wrong way!

> *I call this prospect Corrigan Container for a reason. They were going the wrong way!*

So, after making certain the Five Principles of Consultative Brokerage® are in place—especially the relationship and institutionalization—our valiant Consultative Broker® is ready to make the following presentation.

First, he acknowledges the fact that the client has received the benefit of a softening marketplace.

In the Past 3 Years the Insurance Marketplace Decreased Your Premiums

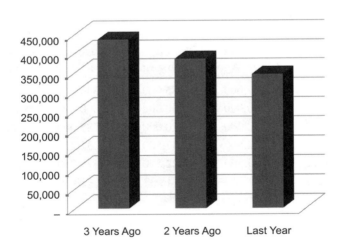

Second, he demonstrates to the prospect how much costs have actually increased by using a Total Cost of Risk Rate.

During the Past 3 Years
Your Costs Increased Each Year!

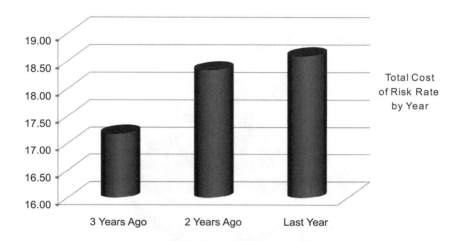

Third, he shows the prospect what the rate difference is over the course of the past two years. In fact, here is where the rubber meets the road. The prospect actually gave back any gain he had received due to the softening of the insurance marketplace.

In the Past 2 Years,
Your Program Gave Back the Gain!

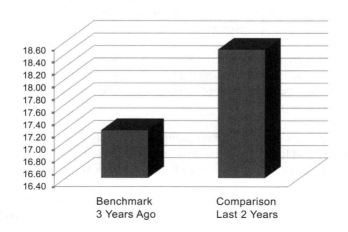

Now, here comes the *coup de grace*, the final nail in the *"we are being well taken care of"* coffin. Based upon the prospect's current profit margins and sales during the past two years, the prospect had to generate additional sales to offset the loss.

In Order to Cover the Expense Increase You Had to Sell More

Cost in Sales
$1,536,228

Total Sales
$59,500,000

See how that worked? Pretty simple eh? Why don't we all create revenue this way? In the event the prospect is a business person, this high level broker has just created a new client. Now the client and the broker can work together in order to really attack the prospect's issues. The focus

The focus becomes reducing the Total Cost of Risk rate.

becomes reducing the Total Cost of Risk rate. This can only be done by bringing in resources and establishing a long-term plan, thereby establishing a business relationship based upon a value proposition.

Just like that great song from the 70s by The Undisputed Truth. While the truth might be in the eyes, it takes focusing the buyer's eyes on the most important factor. Their actual costs. Once you accomplish that, you are home free. The eyes might lie, but the numbers don't!

By the way, this is not a workers compensation only strategy. As we have discussed previously, indirect losses and their impact are felt in all types of loss. The key is to understand the impact of losses on a business and then to quantify it.

We leave this section as we began it: with a word of warning. The concept of TCOR does not sell accounts. It is the vehicle that establishes your credibility. Do not move to the TCOR rate stage until your prospect knows you, trusts you, and understands the focus of your firm. That is the purpose of the five principles. If they are not in place you will simply exchange one commodity (premium) for another (TCOR rate).

Rob's Rule: The TCOR rate is the fuel that drives the value proposition engine.

Chapter 25

The Keys to Consultative Brokerage® Presentations

"It's time to fish or cut bait!"

I started my insurance sales career at the ripe old age of 22, fresh faced and full of vinegar. My first manager was one of the finest men I ever knew in our industry. Frankly, he put up with a lot of nonsense that only a 22-year-old can throw at you. But, he understood that boys will be boys. Anyway, he had an expression I will never forget. It sums it up for all of us.

When the time came to do the deal, he would exclaim, "It's time to fish or cut bait boys!" What did he mean? Well, only one thing. When it is time, let 'em have it with both barrels. Remember, your gun is loaded with value and not sales trickery. So, your presentation should reflect it.

I have seen hundreds of insurance presentations over the years. Most of them are simply schedules of insurance coverage with a back page that contains the prices of coverage. The rest is filler. In fact, many prospects have become so in tune with this that they simply turn to the back page first in order to get to the point.

These are not presentations but simply schedules of insurance with prices attached. They don't move a buyer toward anything other than filling in the blanks of price. They certainly don't complement a sale. A lot of trees have died because of our industry!

Here is what all seasoned consultative brokers know. The sale is created well before the presentation. The presentation merely sums up the conclusions that your firm is ready to present. If you have followed the Consultative Brokerage® strategy to this point, here is what you have accomplished:

The sale is created well before the presentation.

- The buyer has provided you with the data and understands what you are trying to accomplish.

- The buyer trusts your motives and respects your organization.

- The buyer has seen and understands the value of your resources.

- You have uncovered the buyer's issues.

- You have developed a quantitative value proposition.

- You are prepared to present findings that will impact the buyer's financial statement.

Don't throw all this away by making a presentation that looks like everyone else's. You have already won the competition. Now all you need to do is make a presentation that provides the uncomplicated truth.

If you have stayed with us to this point, you have learned that your entire sales strategy hinged on the differentiation of your firm based upon resources and client value. Here is what you did. You put the "fix" in on the transaction. Throughout the sales process, your firm spoke and acted at a higher level. As the buyer became acquainted with your value, you began to separate your firm from the hollow swan songs of the other agents and brokers. While others spoke about their agencies and special insurance programs, you moved the buyer to another level. Also, if the competition included the sleazebag broker or agent (you know who they are in your marketplace) you have already positioned yourself to win.

The Consultative Brokerage Process
Put the Fix In!!!

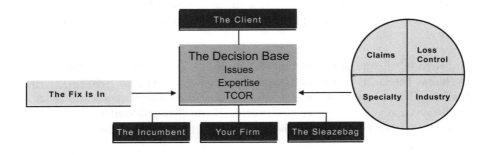

Now it is time for the final step. You must create a presentation that reinforces what you have spent your production time and effort to create: a separation. So, here is what you must deliver to the client in order to create a great presentation. If you have done your homework this is the easy part:

1. **A customized solution.** You should be able to do this through the application of your resources and the TCOR process. This solution must be applied to the client's financial statement.

2. **A theme or themes.** The entire focus of your presentation should be to reinforce the theme or themes of your solutions. If you have positioned the prospect or client correctly this will simply be a restatement of what you have already agreed upon.

3. **Demonstrated expertise.** You will discuss how your firm has accomplished similar successes for other clients. It also will include a restatement of your value proposition (TCOR impact).

4. **Concise verbiage.** Your presentation should get to the point quickly. Let the other brokers spend time on filler. Your presentation is all about one thing: How your firm will help improve the prospect's business.

5. **Visual attractiveness**. Remember that you are providing your prospect and clients with a consultant's report. Make it look that way! Use PowerPoint for the presentation and learn the skills necessary for a quality spoken presentation. If you leave something behind, make it something to be proud of.

6. **Include a call for action.** What is your call for action? Why, being appointed the broker of course. So, the end of your presentation should lead up to only one conclusion . . . that your firm is uniquely qualified to be their broker . . . that choosing you provides the buyer with a great deal of value.

What Makes a Great Presentation

- Customized Solutions
- A Theme or Themes
- Demonstrated Expertise
- Concise Verbiage
- Visual Attractiveness
- A Call for Action

Now all of this may seem complicated. But, actually it isn't. Why? Because, if you have followed the Consultative Brokerage® methodology, you already are prepared. The prospecting process seasoned both you and the prospect for this natural conclusion to your time spent working together. So, in your presentation, you just need to answer these questions. By the way, if you can't answer them, you are not ready to make the presentation.

> *The prospecting process seasoned both you and the prospect for this natural conclusion.*

- What are the issues? You already know these as they became a big part of your value proposition.

- Why are they important? You are in a position to show the buyer how much they are impacting the company's financial statement.

- How is your firm uniquely qualified to solve them? Your resource capabilities will be restated and reconfirmed.

- Who will solve them? By specifically naming the individuals (that hopefully the prospect has already met) you are making an individual commitment.

- When will these be solved? This is the key to your presentation. By providing a timeline, you are giving the prospect something by which to judge your performance.

You *Must* Answer These Questions

- What are the issues?
- Why are they important?
- How is your firm *uniquely* qualified to solve them?
- Who will solve them?
- What are the timeframes?

I think we should spend just a little more time on the last topic of timelines. A successful Consultative Broker® knows the importance of a timeline. This is the call for action and is essentially the last piece of the presentation. The timeline is used to reduce any potential buyer's remorse. It gives the prospect a yardstick by which to measure you. Remember, in the past it was your price. Now, it is your performance. So, provide them with expectations by which to judge you.

> *The timeline is used to reduce any potential buyer's remorse.*

As we have said in the past, expiration dates are fool's gold. Your solutions and client value do not revolve around expiration dates. If that is the case, you must give the prospect another measurement of your performance in the event you intend to be appointed the broker during the policy period. If you intend to fix a problem, when will it be done? That is the moment that your value proposition kicks in.

Here is a very rudimentary example of a timeline. It is a synopsis from an actual account that I was involved in as a working broker. The prospect was a high-tech company that had outgrown its current broker. One of the key issues was the fact that the current broker had provided very little service or value for the prospect's Asian manufacturing operations. We were competing in November for the client's June program renewal. So, as part of our presentation we provided the client with a timeline that provided a yardstick against which to measure our performance.

The Acme Project
Timelines

	Jan	Feb	Mar	Apr	May	June	July
• Appointed as Broker	X						
• Asian Operations Study Done		X					
• Risk Assessment Done		X					
• Insurance Negotiations Done			X				
• Insurance Program Placed				X	X		
• Stewardship Report						X	
• Loss Ctrl. Training	X	X	X	X	X	X	X
• Meetings w/Execs	X	X	X	X	X	X	X

Here is one last important piece that needs to be considered in your presentation. If it is in written form, you need to produce a true executive summary. I have seen many presentations that include what is being passed for an executive summary. In most cases, this executive summary is nothing more than a rehash of the agency/brokerage services.

A true executive summary must be no longer than two pages. It should be placed in the front of the presentation and answer all the questions. It needs to present the theme, the solution, and the impact to the buyer. The last paragraph should answer the questions, "What is the quantifiable benefit to our firm and why should we do business with you?"

Ladies and gentlemen: If you can't boil your presentation and value proposition to two pages, you probably don't have one. The development of an executive summary is where you should begin. Then build your entire presentation around it. The remainder of your presentation is merely providing the data and facts that lead to the conclusions stated in your executive summary.

So, as we close this chapter, there is another universal truth that I would like to leave with you. **The deal is always done before the presentation**. Someone is always in the favorite's role. The principles of Consultative Brokerage® were designed to place you in a position to achieve broker control. It is yours to lose. Don't blow it by making a presentation that looks like everyone else's. You don't need to do that.

Oh, and one other universal truth. The greatest presentation in the world cannot overcome a lack of relationships or a prospect's understanding of your firm. If those pieces are not in place, the prospect will spend time trying to figure out who you are or if they can trust you.

Now you know why we spent such a great deal of time talking about the Principles of Consultative Brokerage®. If you followed these correctly, your proposal is more like a natural conclusion to a project than a onetime event.

> *Your proposal is more like a natural conclusion to a project than a onetime event.*

Rob's Rule: Someone is always in the role of the favorite. Consultative Brokerage® allows you to be that somebody.

Chapter 26

Capability Presentations: The Opening Gambit

"Every crowd has a silver lining."

Phineas Taylor Barnum
US circus showman with James Bailey (1810 – 1891)

S ome brokers call it a Dog & Pony Show. This describes a presentation that is given to a prospect involving a cast of thousands. You know the ones. A broker brings in a team of people to wow the client with their expertise. For forty-five minutes to an hour, the broker wears down the prospect with a startling display of electronic wizardry, lights, moving animation, and skillful verbal description.

Unfortunately, they sometimes miss the mark because they forget one important fact . . . the needs of the prospect, leaving the attendees in startled confusion wondering what was just said. Or, more importantly, what it had to do with them.

Here are some of the client reactions of which you must be aware. When you make a presentation that falls on deaf ears, it is probable that you have triggered one of these client complaints.

The Prospect Says About . . .
Top Complaints of Attendees

- Pressenters didn't know our needs
- Too long; too detailed
- No natural decision step
- Too technical

- Too much about <u>them</u>, not <u>us</u>
- Unclear presentation
- Too much theory
- Too much about what it is, not what it does

In our previous discussions we addressed many of these issues. These complaints are all derived from one common error: the failure of the presenter to do his homework and follow the Consultative Broker® mantra of creating client value. When you focus on the client value, you take the spotlight off yourself. This forces you to see your presentation in a different perspective.

> *When you focus on the client value, you take the spotlight off yourself.*

There are two types of presentations that consultative brokers regularly provide. They are Capability Presentations and Conceptual Proposals. Each of these has a specific purpose; they are not interrelated. Capability presentations are used very early in the prospecting process and are simply an introduction of your firm and its resources. The conceptual proposal is used to provide the prospect your findings and make recommendations as part of the Broker of Record process.

Capability Presentations

A good capability presentation is used to introduce your firm to a prospect or a prospect team. This is merely an introductory tool and sets the stage for the remainder of the process. Sometimes, but very rarely, a prospect will award you the business solely on the capability presentation. But that happens only when something else has occurred inside the transaction. Either the prospect determined her company had outgrown the other broker or she was already sold on your firm.

Capabilities versus Conceptual

Capabilities Presentations	Conceptual Proposals
• The Starting Point	• The Ending Point
• Generic Information	• Specific Conclusions
• Resource Descriptions	• Resource Results
• Impact Created for Others	• Impact Created for Prospect
• Goal – Gather Data	• Goal – Appoint as Broker

So, for our purposes let's discuss how a solid capabilities presentation is used to set the stage for Consultative Brokerage® and build the beginnings of a value platform. Remember this: a capabilities presentation is not the end game, but only the beginning.

A successful Consultative Broker® uses the capabilities presentation as a method of separating himself from the competition. It is also a barometer to determine the temperature of the prospect. If the prospect is interested and interactive, a broker knows she is making progress.

So the initial sales strategy that leads up to the capabilities presentation is a simple interest in introducing your firm to the prospect. This introduction includes further acquainting the prospect with your capabilities. Don't forget, capabilities without benefits are meaningless. Don't fall into the trap of providing the prospect with a list of your features. The buyer will not be attracted by this.

Here are the parts of a first class capabilities presentation.

1. Your firm introduction – Keep this quick and simple. Show the prospect your history and indicate some of the key players. But don't make this the centerpiece of your presentation because this is all about you.

2. Your business philosophy – This is the part that involves the introduction of the TCOR philosophy. Show the prospect how your firm is committed to helping your clients reduce their costs. Make certain you understand the importance of the symmetry of risk and how indirect loss costs impact their business model.

   Make certain you understand the importance of the symmetry of risk and how indirect loss costs impact their business model.

3. Your resource capabilities – Unveil your resource capabilities as an adjunct to your business philosophy of client cost reduction and value. Emphasize that these resources are your firm's investment in the guaranteed outcome.

4. Your impact on other clients – Show the prospect how your TCOR philosophy, when coupled with your resources, has reduced other clients' costs. Give several examples of how your clients have experienced quantifiable impact on their financial statements.

5. Your call for action – Provide the prospect with an action plan that emphasizes a common goal of value and cost reduction. In many cases the action item will be the agreement to provide you the data required to truly understand the prospect's current Total Cost of Risk.

Many firms create one capabilities presentation and show it to all their prospects. In the event you choose this route, I recommend that you create a module for Section 4 that can be modified for use with various industry groups. For instance, the impact you have on a construction account may be somewhat different than a healthcare account. So, take the time to make it industry specific.

Here is one word of caution on capabilities presentations. When you create them, you must build in points that will allow for open discussion with the prospect. Many times we fall into the trap of creating such a powerful presentation that we forget to include the audience. So, as you create and present your capabilities presentation make certain that you consider these issues:

- How have our capabilities assisted other firms like this prospect?

- How do we involve a prospect to discuss ways our capabilities can be applied to his team and company?

- What is the action item of our presentation?

- What will we do if the prospect does not seem interested or interactive?

The last question is one that all successful consultative brokers eventually face. They are putting their best stuff on the table and some in the audience seem less than receptive. In some cases the response could even be defined as "frosty".

When this occurs, it will be important for the presenter to slow down the presentation and ask the reluctant participant if there are any issues that are of concern. This question will uncover a number of bumps in the road that must be removed. The participants' body language will always reveal their true feelings. Pay particular importance to this, as failure to address this now will lead to derailment of your sales strategy later. (After you have invested a great deal of time and effort!)

Capabilities presentations are a very professional way to introduce your firm at a high level to begin the sales process. They set the stage for gathering data and prospect cooperation that ultimately leads to a conceptual proposal and the Broker of Record appointment.

Rob's Rule: Capabilities presentations are the opening gambit to the creation of a Consultative Brokerage® sale.

Chapter 27

Conceptual Presentations: The Grand Finale

"Carpe Diem! Seize the Day!"

From a Latin poem by Horace (*Odes* 1.11)

The major difference between the Capabilities Presentation and a Conceptual Proposal is the direct application of resources, specific recommendations, and proposed results that you present based upon your research. This research is based upon the data of the client and how your resources will be deployed to reduce costs.

As a neophyte broker I am ashamed to say that my first "conceptual" presentation was a complete dud. Oh, it was not from lack of effort, merely ignorance of Consultative Brokerage®.

I had been invited by a major account to present a conceptual proposal about how we would address the company's risk management costs. I made the cardinal mistake of substituting the term risk financing (i.e., insurance) for risk management.

Armed with all the necessary data on losses and risk control, I proceeded to get to work. When we were done, I had created one of the great masterpieces of all time that showed how the prospect's program could be designed through utilization of deductibles, various retros, self-insurance, and captive programs. This diatribe was worthy of any textbook on the subject of "How to design insurance programs." It should have been; I copied it from all of them.

Of course we didn't get the business. I had missed the point entirely. The client wasn't interested in our knowledge about how to place insurance. He assumed we knew that. He was concerned about how we would apply our intellectual capital to help the company reduce costs.

He was concerned about how we would apply our intellectual capital to help the company reduce costs.

A conceptual proposal is used to demonstrate to a prospect your specific solution along with your impact on Total Cost of Risk. It is called *conceptual* for a reason: The prospect is asked to make a decision based upon how your *concepts* will apply to her company.

Again, that is the purpose of working the Consultative Brokerage® Principles. A prospect will not believe your *concepts* unless he is convinced you really understand his issues and that he knows you. If those pieces are not in place, he will turn to the decision base he is familiar with . . . price of the commodity.

So, be very careful here. You have one chance to make a conceptual proposal and you need to make certain that the prospect is ready. Here are the things you must confirm before making your conceptual presentation:

1. Will all the prospect decision makers be in the meeting? This is critical as your presentation will involve some quantifiable value. This value should not be translated through others. You need the ability to look everyone in the eye as you unleash your strongest material.

2. Do you have the right data? You must confirm prior to the meeting that nothing has changed regarding the loss data or loss control program. If things have improved, your presentation is obsolete and will be discounted. If they are worse, your presentation and its conclusion become even stronger.

3. Are you seeing the prospect's costs correctly? You must confirm that the prospect's cost base is correct. In the case of indirect loss costs it is imperative that the prospect has agreed beforehand not only that these costs exist, but at what factor. (i. e., how much does each loss cost)? You cannot spend your time in the meeting justifying the cost base you are using. If so, your presentation will disintegrate.

4. Will the client be ready to make a decision? In many cases, a conceptual proposal is delivered in mid-policy period. Our industry has usually made expiration dates the arbitrary time of decision. You must confirm that the prospect will appoint you in the event your firm provides value, regardless of the expiration date.

All of the above questions are the same ones a consulting firm would ask before delivering its opinions and proposals for the project. You have the same rights and responsibilities. I say responsibilities because you are leading a team. That team depends upon you as the broker for leadership. Don't lead them into uncharted waters.

There are several other things you should do prior to the big day of the conceptual proposal:

1. Practice the presentation. If you intend to involve a number of people, make certain they all know their parts.

2. Prepare backup materials. Have an extra copy of the presentation on disk and bring an extra computer to the meeting.

3. Know the exact location of the meeting. There are some firms that have several locations or campus-type settings. Make sure you know the exact location if you are presenting at one of the prospect's locations.

4. Double check all of the presentation materials. At the end of the day it is your responsibility to make certain everything is correct. Unless you are planning to give the word processing department a cut of the commission, you need to take the ultimate responsibility for accuracy.

Now some of these tips may seem rather rudimentary. But let me tell you a little story about how I learned some of them the hard way.

I had been asked to make a presentation to the board of a major New York corporation. This particular firm had two Wall Street addresses. One was the main corporate location and the second was a divisional office. I was invited to speak to the board at the corporate office.

I arrived at the corporate office in plenty of time. Upon entering the massive reception area I announced myself to the receptionist and expected to hear Gabriel's Trumpet at my arrival. Unfortunately, here is what I heard instead. "I am sorry Mr. Ekern, but the meeting you were expected to attend was yesterday." SAY WHAT?

Well, you can imagine my response. (Once I stopped quivering.) Thank goodness a second receptionist overheard the conversation. "Oh, no," she replied, "that meeting is today. In fact they are meeting now and expect you shortly."

Whew, that was a close one. Problem solved. Until she dropped the next bomb, "They are meeting at our divisional office location four blocks away." Oh, did I tell you that it was also raining?

So, there I was, with a briefcase in one hand and a suit bag slung across my shoulder dodging the puddles on Wall Street at a full sprint. Quite a sight as my wool suit clung to my body. But, I made it in time.

Once again, a receptionist, but this time the results were different. After a quick spritz in the men's room I heard the magic words, "Go on in Mr. Ekern, they are expecting you."

This was the moment I had been waiting for. I had spent several days in preparation and had my presentation placed on overhead transparencies. (Ok, it was in the early 90s before PowerPoint.) It was beautiful!

I confidently strode into the room and took my place at the front of the polished mahogany table. Large and in charge. Until I realized that no one had obtained an overhead projector. So, I stood in front of this group and held up my beautiful transparencies and explained what they should be seeing. All the while, the CFO was rummaging in a closet looking for a projector. Nobody heard a word I said. Not my finest moment.

The Conceptual Proposal is your moment to shine. *Carpe Diem*! (Seize the Day!) Let the other brokers make a presentation based upon the same worn out material that they have used over and over again. It is your turn to make a presentation that hits the prospect where she lives, her financial statement and your ability to improve it.

Here are the steps you must cover in your Consultative Brokerage® conceptual presentation:

1. A brief history of your firm and your interaction with the prospect to date. This is important as there may be some people in the room who are not familiar with you and how you came to be involved.

2. Your theme of TCOR and how it impacts buyers. This is not a primer on TCOR; by this time the client should have a complete understanding.

3. Your identification of the issues that are (or could) create financial leakage. These must be shown to the prospect in a quantifiable manner. This becomes your benchmark of value.

4. An introduction of your specific resources and how they will be specifically applied to reduce the prospect's costs. This will be done through the application of the four quadrants of resources.

5. The financial impact of achieving your goals compared to the current benchmark of the prospect.

6. A timeline for implementation and achievement. This is very important for the reasons already discussed. It removes potential buyer's remorse.

7.   A brief review of the insurance marketplace. The purpose of this is to show the prospect your ability to represent his company inside the insurance marketplace. The main point should be your ability to access the primary markets.

8.   Ask for the business! This is the ultimate call to action. By this time, you and your organization should have separated yourselves from the pack. If the cake ain't baked by now, it will never be ready.

When you make a quality conceptual proposal you must remember one thing. You are not making an insurance sales presentation. You have just finished a consulting project, so act like it. Stand tall, present with confidence, and demonstrate to your prospect why you and your organization have the intellectual capital to represent her best interests.

You have just finished a consulting project, so act like it.

Rob's Rule: A conceptual presentation is a consultant's report. A consultant and an insurance agent are two different things!

Chapter 28

Stewardship Reports

"Give a man a fish and you feed him for a day. Teach a man to fish and you feed him for a lifetime."

Chinese Proverb

No conversation about Consultative Brokerage® presentations would be complete without a discussion concerning Stewardship Reports. This type of presentation is the most effective way I know to secure your current renewal book. Unfortunately, while many brokers talk about them, very few actually provide them to clients on a consistent basis.

It happens several times a year. I get the call from a very frustrated broker. "I've really got a problem," he moans, "My biggest account is under attack by one of my toughest competitors." The beleaguered broker goes on to whine, "And what's worse is that my client gave away all the good markets. What should I do?"

The broker usually goes silent when I ask him the tough question. "How did your stewardship report go?"

After several seconds of pregnant pause, I hear the muffled reply, "I didn't do one." Followed by a hushed question, "Do you think I should have?"

DO I THINK YOU SHOULD HAVE? My friend you are now in a competition that could have been completely avoided if you had taken the time to provide your biggest client with a stewardship report.

So, in answer to his first question of what to do next, here is my usual reply. "Get under your desk in the fetal position because now you are in a dogfight. Even if you retain this account you will be a loser because the other broker will do everything possible to make your life miserable and probably a lot less profitable."

Here is the sad truth. Most large accounts end up in competition because the holding broker saw her role simply as that of an insurance provider. The incumbent didn't do a stewardship report because she couldn't talk about anything other than how well her firm had placed the insurance and how the carrier paid claims. Or, sadly, she didn't do one because she saw it as needless work. So, she ended up having to work even harder to try to keep the renewal client!

A quality stewardship report is the only way I know to take the sting out of the renewal. As most of you know, once a renewal competition starts, everyone is an adversary. You are competing against the other broker, the other carriers (most of whom you represent), and in some cases your own client.

> *A quality stewardship report is the only way I know to take the sting out of the renewal.*

So, here is how to avoid it and keep your revenues up without being mauled by everyone in the process. Do a stewardship report on your Franchise Accounts . . . period!

The timing of stewardship reports is very important. I always recommend that stewardship reports be presented six months into the renewal period. Why six months? Because that is a time when there is no pressure on the renewal. This is the time when you have the ability to focus on your accomplishments without making it entirely about the insurance marketplace. Also, you want to make certain you present it before the hoards of price-selling brokers descend upon your client. Hopefully, you will provide your client with the ammunition necessary to stave off these locusts.

There are, however, other times when generating a stewardship report is very important. The main one is the situation when a new CFO, risk manager, or owner shows up on the scene. It is critical that these new players understand your complete value proposition and long-term commitment before they attempt to throw you to the wolves of competition.

Here are the main purposes of a stewardship report:

1. To solidify your value proposition. At least once a year your client needs to be reminded that your firm is more than simply an insurance agency. That your firm and you, in particular, have played an important role in the business operations. Even the most loyal client needs to hear this before his phone begins to ring with the price seller's siren song.

2. To discuss client expectations. It is important that both you and your client discuss the expectations of each other at a time when the pressure of the

renewal is not in play. Have we done what the client expected of us? Has the client held up her end of the bargain in regard to the implementation of loss control programs?

3. To build additional relationships. Your stewardship report may include participants from both the client side and from your side who have not been involved previously. For example, sometimes the client will involve other senior executives who have not been in the insurance buying process. Therefore, a stewardship report is a great way to attract new players to your value camp.

4. To create client confidence in the decision to hire you. One of the best ways to do this is to identify not only the projects you have completed but also to identify future issues that must be addressed through additional projects. (If you run out of projects you will find yourself in a price/commodity transaction.)

5. To set up the renewal. One of the main reasons for a stewardship report is to test the waters regarding the client's wishes for the renewal. Does it surprise you to learn that in many cases, we create our own competition because we fail to provide the client with information? By doing a complete stewardship report, we now have the right to expect the client to continue to do business with us.

What is the Purpose of a Stewardship Report?

- Solidify Value
- Discuss Expectations
- Build Relations
- Identify Future Issues
- Set Up the Renewal

Move Into **Charted** Waters!

If only we all did them on our largest accounts! What a difference it would make. Not only would we be doing ourselves a world of good, but imagine the impact to our industry. If every client began to hear a story regarding our value, the perception of us as an industry would change. We would not constantly be expected to

> *If every client began to hear a story regarding our value, the perception of us as an industry would change.*

be the most *competitive* (i.e., cheapest) insurance providers. Oh well, that is my dream, but you as a broker don't need to share it, just take care of your own clients the way you should. Do those stewardship reports!

I am constantly asked for a copy of a good stewardship report. I never have provided one. Why? Because the moment I give one out, it will become the industry standard on various word processing equipment across North America. Eventually, it would find its way onto one of the accounting software platforms that hold themselves out as insurance proposal generation tools. The result would be a product that is inferior because it does not fit the exact specifications of each client.

If you catch fish for a person they will eat for one day. But, if you teach a person to fish, they will feed themselves forever. Are you ready to go fishing?

Here are the six specific issues that your stewardship report must address. Remember that simply a list of your services is not enough. It is critical that you demonstrate to the client how you applied them and will continue to on the client's behalf.

Stewardship Reports:
The 6 Sections to Success

- Brief Introduction
- Service Review
- Demonstration of Value
- Future Projects and Goals
- Marketplace Review
- Obtain Validation

1. A brief background of your firm. Once again, it is not necessary that you overwhelm the buyer with information about your organization. The purpose of the meeting is them! But, there may be some attendees who have not been exposed to your organization previously. So, provide enough to get them up to speed.

2. A review of the projects your firm has completed over the course of the past eighteen months. Why eighteen months? Because you want to show a long-term commitment without talking about ancient history. Also, you should list at least three projects you have completed that provide value outside of the insurance transaction.

3. A demonstration of value. Your presentation must show the client how your firm provided quantifiable value during the eighteen-month stewardship period. It is important that the client understand how your projects have impacted the company's financial statements. Use the TCOR method to do this.

4. Future projects and goals. The stewardship report identifies the projects your firm will tackle over the course of the next eighteen months and how the client will benefit. Once again use the conceptual portion of a Consultative Brokerage® presentation to demonstrate your value. Why eighteen months? Because it gets you past the next renewal date. If your client is acknowledging this value, it is full steam ahead. If, on the other hand, the client is sitting with arms crossed, you need to slow down. What is this body language telling you?

5. A brief marketplace review. While the stewardship report does not focus primarily on the insurance, it is important that you provide your client with a window of expectations. This will defuse the need in their minds to involve other brokers who are singing the price mantra. You must simply assure the client that when the time comes in several months, you will provide a complete marketplace report and discuss the renewal project.

6. Obtain validation. This is the most important part. Your client must validate the value that your firm has provided. Also, you must have an understanding on how you will be moving forward over the course of the next eighteen months. If you don't get this, you may find yourself in a competition down the road. It is imperative that you move forward as partners rather than as adversaries.

> *It is imperative that you move forward as partners rather than as adversaries.*

It is my opinion that virtually every brokerage competition could have been avoided if the holding broker had done a stewardship report. At the very least, the incumbent would have known the lay of the land prior to the competition beginning. But, alas, they are not done very often or very well. So, the poor broker is forced to compete for his own account. Wouldn't it be better to prove your value while you are still in control?

Rob's Rule: If you don't do a stewardship report, you don't deserve to hold the renewal.

Conclusion

"Today my jurisdiction ends here."

John Cleese as Sheriff John Langston in the movie *Silverado*

W ell, there you have it. I said I wouldn't pull any punches in these pages and I hope you agree that I didn't. Frankly, we could go on a lot longer. If so, we would discuss how to implement a Consultative Brokerage® program, how to lead a Consultative Brokerage® sale or ways to attract Consultative Brokerage® clients. In addition we would go deeper into the discussion of Total Cost of Risk and ways to judge your effectiveness with a client. Perhaps we will address some of those issues in upcoming books.

But, for today, my jurisdiction ends here.

I sincerely hope that some of you may decide to delve deeper into the world of Consultative Brokerage®. It is the only way you will prosper inside our industry. Hard or soft marketplace, evolving client expectations, and a widening definition of risk are all things many of you will deal with over the coming years. The methodology of Consultative Brokerage® is the only way you can slow down the moving parts long enough to build and retain a substantial book of business.

> *Consultative Brokerage®*
> *is the only way you*
> *can slow down the*
> *moving parts long*
> *enough to build and*
> *retain a substantial*
> *book of business.*

So, if I haven't convinced you by now, here are some closing thoughts on why virtually all of you must make the changes necessary to work as a Consultative Broker®:

1. Your clients and prospects will grow to expect it.

2. Your carriers will not be able to sustain growth by the antiquated competition method.

3. Your firms will require a substantial ROI for the investment in resources.

4. You must value your production time effectively.

5. It is a heck of a lot more fun!

The first time you try and work this way you will feel like you are jumping off a cliff. You will not have the safety net of using carriers as your main source of competition. So, stay firm and do not take the path of least resistance (i.e., Marketplace Competition). There may not be anyone who will reinforce your business methodology. It will feel lonely at first because you are blazing a new trail. Your competitors will not reinforce this because they want you to compete on price. Your carriers may not reinforce it because it doesn't focus entirely around them. Lastly, your prospects may be confused because they are used to creating a bidding environment. Therefore, they will attempt to pull you into the tangled web of marketplace competition.

It will be up to you to operate at a higher level and not attempt to use Consultative Brokerage® as merely a "sales technique." It is a business model that will allow you and your respective firms to maintain a value platform based upon differentiation. To achieve this you must be single-minded concerning your implementation and client service approach. This is a business culture that you can replicate throughout your firm and book of business.

One more word of advice: Don't fall into the trap of using Consultative Brokerage® on a selected basis. Rather than adapting your value proposition and business methodology on a prospect by prospect basis, use your time to find a series of prospects that will all respond to Consultative Brokerage®. The key to success in any business is finding enough prospects that will respond in a predictable manner.

> *The key to success in any business is finding enough prospects that will respond in a predictable manner.*

Remember, they can shoot ya' but they can't eat ya'. So, if a prospect is not responding to you, simply find another one. You just don't have to waste your time on every prospect that is not willing to save his company from the death spiral of price and commodity. Eventually, even those prospects will run out of steam . . . and then what?

So, as you move forward in your respective careers, I sincerely hope that this book will help many of you. You have a choice. Will you base your production careers and firms on something you can't control, or will you focus on establishing your own unique value proposition?

I trust you know my recommendation on that matter!

Best regards from all Consultative Brokers®.

C. R. (Rob) Ekern

> *Will you base your production careers and firms on something you can't control, or will you focus on establishing your own unique value proposition?*

Appendix A

A Word to Carriers

I know what some of you carrier reps are thinking after reading this book: "Hey, this guy is really giving us a hard time. If all our agents worked this way, we would be in trouble. Broker-of-record letters are not good for us."

I have heard it all. Some carriers have indicated that this methodology, especially as it relates to broker-of-record letters, is dangerous. "It doesn't take into account the special relationships with some brokers that we have established." Or, "We resist broker-of-record letters because they don't create growth for our shareholders"—i.e., new business to us.

None of these arguments takes into account the greatly reduced cost of working with an agent or broker who is prepared to place the account with you, rather than forcing you to bid your own renewal. An agent or broker who knows how to deliver value using the resources in which your shareholders have invested.

We have a brokerage client who has recently been criticized by some of its carrier partners because submission flow has really decreased. Why? Because this broker is working exclusively on a broker-of-record basis. The producers have a hit ratio of over 80 percent on the deals they work on and don't use the marketplace as their price-stalking horse.

So, why don't we all get on the same page? The most expensive thing you do is quote business. This is especially true in a softening marketplace. Eventually you face the same problems as your broker clients. Your profit ratios erode due to price competition. Then, we all run on the same gerbil treadmill, eventually collapsing in exhaustion.

Over the course of the past years I have been involved in meetings of the highest level with carriers, brokers, and clients. We all ask the same questions from a different perspective. "How can we create the most cost effective programs?"

Unfortunately, in many cases we take the position that cost effectiveness revolves around price. The concept of a three-legged stool (carriers, brokers, and clients) goes out the window under the banner of *negotiation*. This happens when all parties to the transaction focus primarily on the commodity to protect what is perceived as their respective best interests.

I have never spoken to a carrier representative who did not agree with the concept of *differentiation*. They all agree that, in order to survive and prosper, they must work with agents who know how to create and deliver a value proposition other than price. But, how do they accomplish this?

First of all, select the agents who best understand how to differentiate themselves. Look for the firms that have made a commitment to the investment in and understanding of resource capabilities. Then align your resource capabilities in a quantifiable support position that can be identified as creating value for the client and the agent. This is entirely a different focus from providing *inspectors* to support underwriting decisions.

Spend the time necessary to establish what your value proposition really is. Then provide your production plant with the tools to present it to agents and clients. Be steadfast in your transition from a pure underwriting organization to a firm that is committed to client cost reduction. As you provide these resources to firms that understand how to use them, your underwriting picture will improve.

You must understand why your best agents have invested money in their own resources. Support these firms. They are not in an adversarial position with you. Once you understand how to interface with them your partnership will strengthen where it matters—at the client service level.

Look, I know some of these issues are difficult to implement at a carrier level. It will require a cultural change inside your organization. However, the carriers that we have worked with in the implementation of a Consultative Brokerage® support strategy are reporting a significant improvement in client retention and agent satisfaction. Why? Because, now they are speaking from the same hymnal of a *value proposition*. Their brokers understand how to differentiate it, the clients understand how to value it, and these carriers know how to deliver it. Now the three-legged stool is intact.

So, I sincerely hope that your respective organizations will discover the importance of seeking out and supporting members of your agency or brokerage plants who understand how to work as consultative brokerages. At the time of this writing, firms that control over $500 million of commissions and fees are working from the Consultative Brokerage® platform. That translates to over $5 billion of **your** premiums.

Why not come along?

Appendix B

A Word to Smaller Agencies

A common misunderstanding is that Consultative Brokerage® is a platform for only large agencies and brokerages. And that it only applies to large accounts. While it is true that the expenses related to the investment in specialized resources may exceed the budget of smaller firms, the need is the same. In addition, while some of the accounts may be smaller, to a small account the impact of indirect losses are proportionately greater expenses.

So, how do you fill this need? Very simple. Establish strong relationships with the carriers who have the resources and understand how to utilize them. In some cases your best carriers will have all the resources you need—with one little twist. Make certain your carrier understands that you need to demonstrate a value proposition to your clients and prospects.

The next time one of your company marketing reps calls on your firm ask this question: "What resources do you have that we can utilize to reduce our clients costs?" Or, when they tell you about the new program they are offering that includes pricing and coverage, follow-up with this: "In addition to the underwriting programs, how can we deploy your loss control resources and claims management to help our clients improve their balance sheets?"

I am not trying to throw a hand grenade into your carrier relationships, but if they can't provide you with resources to help both of you provide value, then each of you is in trouble. Eventually another carrier and agent will come up with a better commodity-based mousetrap.

So, ask the value questions and understand how to translate that information to prospects and clients. Make certain that your clients and prospects know that, while the other agents are merely purveyors of price and commodity, you understand how to access the resources of the carrier. Thereby you differentiate yourself and your carrier partner.

There is another strategy of which you should be aware. I call it the *spheres of resource* approach. You can obtain many of the resources you need for larger accounts from third parties. For instance, virtually all of the major adjusting companies will provide you access to third party administrator and claims expertise. There are several loss control firms that contract out their services to agents and brokers. In addition, whether it is forensic accountants (for business interruption claims) or London-based wholesalers, you can replicate virtually any service provided by a mega-broker. You just need to know where to look and how to deploy these resources.

So, as a final word to a smaller firm: Don't fold your hand when running into a larger account or larger competition. Simply understand ways to work as a Consultative Broker® and focus on the how and why of resource capabilities that are already available to you.